STORYTELLING WITH THE
FLANNEL BOARD

STORYTELLING WITH THE FLANNEL BOARD

by DR. PAUL S. ANDERSON
San Diego State College

Art Work by MISS IRENE FRANCIS
Teacher, National City, California

Publishers
T. S. DENISON & COMPANY, INC.

 **Publishers SINCE 1876**   T. S. DENISON & COMPANY, INC.

Standard Book Number: 513-00105-0
Library of Congress Card Number: 62-21650
Printed in the United States of America

CONTENTS

*Dedicated to the students in the elementary teacher
training program at San Diego State College
who have told these stories.*

Acknowledgements

Many individuals and groups have contributed to this material. As with folk literature some of these stories have been passed on from teacher to teacher through the years until it is no longer possible to identify the originator.

Special arrangements have been made in order to include the following stories.

"Apron Calendar" by Lucy Elder appeared in Child Life Magazine in January 1955 and "Wee Ann" by Leila Browne appeared in the same magazine in December 1954.

"Tommy Turkey" is reprinted by permission of the Webster Publishing Co. from *Talking Time* by Louise Bender Scott and J. J. Thompson. Copyright 1951 by Webster Publishing Co.

"The Little Rabbit Who Wanted Red Wings" by Carolyn Sherwin Bailey is used with the permission of the publisher, Plutt and Munk.

"The Giraffe Who Went to School" by Irma Wilde is from Read Aloud Kindergarten Stories. Copyright 1957 by Winden Books, Inc.

"Florry Skywriter" by Mabel Watts is republished with their permission by the author and Winden Books, Inc.

"Gerry Goose," "Carrie Kangaroo," "Spring Story" are used with the permission of Appleton Century Crofts, Inc. and are from *Speech Disorders, Principles and Practices of Therapy* by Mildred F. Berry and Jon Eisensen, Copyright 1956.

Chapter 1

Storytelling with the Flannel Board

When Hans Christian Andersen entertained the children of Denmark with his stories, he used to cut out silhouettes in order to make the characters more vivid. In ancient China, the storyteller would cast shadows to illustrate the characters in his tales of magic and ancient ways. The modern movie cartoon favorites, such as Mr. Magoo, use a combination of silhouette figures and movement to hold attention. In the modern classroom, the flannelgraph provides the storyteller the means to achieve the same movement, characterization and magic.

As the child listens to the storyteller, his visual attention is focused on characters and movement while figures are moved about on the flannel board. These figures are simple outline representations of the main characters which are cut out. On the back of each item used, the storyteller has pasted a bit of flannel or sandpaper so that it will adhere to a board covered with flannel.

As a part of the training program in the last war, flannelgraph was used to illustrate troop movements, traffic control problems and map reading in much the same manner as a sand table might be used. The flannel board has the advantage of being upright so that a class can watch it in the same way that they would use a blackboard.

When I returned from the services, my work involved supervision of some county schools. One day in early October I planned to visit a first grade room. A visit by a stranger can be disturbing to children this early in

7

the year, and teachers seldom feel at ease during the first visit of a supervisor. I tried to think of something that could be offered to both teacher and children that might ease tension. Since Halloween was approaching, the story "Queer Company" came to my mind. At noon while waiting for the class to assemble, I cut out crude figures to go with the story. A nearby store provided a yard of light-blue outing flannel which was soon fastened to one side of a large cardboard packing box.

What the teacher thought when I appeared with all this equipment is unknown but she probably had some doubts. At any rate, I explained that I would like to tell a story to the children before observing their regular classroom activities. We visited about the Halloween decorations that were in evidence, and the children told about anticipated fun on Halloween. It was agreed that it was fun to scare people if they knew it was "just pretend." Then the children listened to the story with the engrossed attention and enthralled response that is a storyteller's greatest reward. As the story ended, a child immediately pleaded, "Tell it again." This time various children were asked to help in placing the characters on the board at the appropriate time. Later their interest led to several of their own retellings in other classrooms.

It is probably all right now to admit that I needed something to give me additional security during this first visit of supervision. This is one more of the values of the flannelgraph. Although it requires time and practice to prepare the right figures, they serve as an outline to follow that makes the storytelling easier. Then, too, some beginners need something tangible, such as these figures, to hold in their hands when they work before an audience. A flannelgraph story is about as foolproof an experience as any that can be suggested for a beginning teacher. A friendly response and personal acceptance by the children of a new teacher makes such a difference in further teaching attempts.

The stories here are favorites that lend themselves to flannel-board presentation. The best stories for use on a flannel board are those that follow a repetitive refrain, those that have one major plot with no subplots, those that contain the kind of action that can be illustrated by figures on the board and can be told with a reasonable number of figures. The old stories which involve magic are especially good. The frog can change into a prince. The objects the king touches can turn to gold. The fish can swallow the tin soldier.

Many modern books such as those by Marjorie Flack or Virginia Lee Burton could be told with the use of the flannelgraph. However, the illustrations in these books are a value in themselves and should be shared with children. Marjorie Flack achieves so much suspense through her illustrations that they are an essential part of the story. Children relive these stories as they take a book and follow page by page even though they cannot read the words. There is a picture sequence that is readable. For these reasons such stories should be kept with the book rather than used for storytelling.

Another type of book that should not be used in flannelgraph presentation is the type that children can read for themselves. Of course, "Nobody Listened to Andrew"[1] would be a delightful story told by the teacher but it is a mistake to exploit such material that can be discovered by the young reader needing materials to challenge and nurture his newly acquired reading ability.

Flannelgraph stories should be looked upon as a means of stimulating the imagination and improving the quality of oral language of children. Many teachers find that permitting children to make their own flannelgraph stories and telling them helps children grow in language power, self-confidence and releases creative talents. Another aspect is the emotional release that can be observed in some children as they plan, cut out and manipulate figures to go with some story they especially like or that they create.

In addition to storytelling, the flannel board has many other classroom uses. Fractional parts in arithmetic can be illustrated and combined. Maps can be made with overlays of rivers, mountains and subdivisions. Almost any idea that would make a good bulletin board can be planned on a flannel board. Music notes can be moved around with ease as music is created.

[1]Guilfoile, E.: Nobody Listened to Andrew, Follett Pub. Co., Chicago, 1957

Games can be explained with the movement of various players illustrated. There are references listed later that will help you discover other ways in which this "magic board" can be used.

While the term flannel board is used here one may be made with felt or coat lining. Those made for children's games are sometimes sprayed with "flocking." A store that specializes in window display materials will have this for sale. If flannel is used, get the heaviest available. Coat lining is usually obtainable from a J. C. Penney, or Sears store. If you have a large bulletin board which you wish to cover, use felt or coat lining. This will cost about ten or twelve dollars. Each figure needs to have a large piece of flannel or felt glued to the reverse side. Then as it is placed on the board the teller should run his finger over the figure. This causes it to adhere to the board. Some use rough sandpaper on the figures or flocking. My experience is that sandpaper makes the figure too heavy and that flocking wears off. For some figures bits of flannel about an inch square in three or four places serve to hold better than one large piece.

Children seem to respond to figures made of bright and heavy construction paper better than those that are drawn. Apparently these allow more play for the imagination. However, illustrations cut from books and made into figures for the flannel board also appeal to them. In a sense, this type simply transfers the book illustrations to the flannel board. Faces and clothes can be drawn with ink, wax crayon or made of bits of construction paper pasted to the figure. The outline of story characters that appear later in this book may be traced or cut out and colored.

Some stories need a change of scenery—a big woods, a lake, a castle. Rather than make these of paper it is easiest to draw them with crayon on a large piece of flannel. Then the figures will stick to the scenery as the story is told. Regular outing flannel that costs about forty-nine cents a yard is good for this purpose.

Most flannel boards are made of plywood or heavy composition cardboard about two feet wide and three feet long. The felt or flannel should be about three feet by four feet in order to allow an adequate overlap on the back of the plywood. Staples from a regular paper stapler will hold it well. Do not try to glue the flannel to the board. This usually lessens the static electricity which causes the figures to adhere. The size should be large enough to hold the figures of these stories but not so large that it is uncomfortable to carry or awkward to store away. Some like to have handles on a board, others hinge them so they will fold. It costs about as much to make a board as to buy one. The only advantage to a homemade one is that you have exactly what you want.

Guidelines for the Storyteller

There are no basic rules to insure the proper telling of a story. Some of the greatest of the story craftsmen cannot agree as to the best methods to use. Storytelling is as individual an art as acting or playing a musical instrument. Each person must develop his own techniques, style and selection of stories to suit his taste and abilities.

There are a few basic considerations, however, upon which most storytellers agree. First, the story must be appropriate to the audience. The very young child likes simple folk tales, but he does not respond to stories that are completely make-believe with goblins, elves and fairies. He does not understand the completely abstract. There must be some elements in the story that relate to his personal experiences. In the story of "The Three Bears" we have chairs, beds, bowls of soup and activities which are familiar. Having them associated with bears adds mystery and adventure but the events are familiar everyday experiences. He accepts the unreal because it is close enough to the real world he knows.

Little children love rhymes and jingles and many old story favorites have a marked rhythmic quality. In stories this rhythm is the result of repetition of words and phrases in a set pattern. Such phrases as "Not by the hair of your chinny-chin-chin," or "Then I'll huff and I'll puff and I'll blow your house in," always bring delighted responses.

Children like to play with words. That is the way words become more meaningful and a lasting part of their vocabulary. Children cannot keep from repeating "a lovely, light luscious delectable cake" as the teacher reads "The Duchess Bakes a Cake."[2] In telling some stories, the teller prepares the listeners by saying, "This story contains some wonderful new words. One of them is —————— which means ——————; another is —————— which means ——————, etc. Listen for them."

Make-believe is most important to children in the years from six to ten since it helps them understand the world about them and increases their

---

[2]Kahl, V.: The Duchess Bakes a Cake. Scribner, N. Y., 1955

imaginative powers. In the stories that they read and hear, the youngsters are the heroes—at least for the time being. They know they are pretending, but as the story unfolds each boy is Jack the Giant Killer and each girl is Cinderella.

Joseph Lee says in his book, "Play in Education,"[3] "Myths and fairy stories, sketching in rainbow colors man's spiritual demands, with a royal disregard of physical limitations, are to the child a rough draft of his future deeds. We must feed the imagination and allow it scope if we would have the child grow up. Imagination is the first step in the life process, it is the material out of which all achievement is condensed."

Second, the storyteller knows that some stories are good to tell—other stories are better to read. A story for telling must be simple and direct. The plot must be strong and develop rapidly. In storytelling there is no place for long analysis of characters or situations. The mental pictures must be supplied by a few words or a phrase. Each incident must be vivid and clear-cut in the listener's mind. The climax must be emotionally satisfying. This can be a surprise, the solution of a problem, or something achieved.

"The Three Little Pigs" is an example of a good story to tell little children. Each step is an event. No time is spent in explanation or unnecessary description. The story tells what the characters did and said and the events are the links of a sequence of the closest kind. There are no breaks and no complexities of plot. Each event makes a clear distinct picture for the imagination.

Ordinarily it is wisest not to change traditional stories. If you question any element in a story it is usually best to select another story. There is a trend in the direction of removing much of the horror aspects of the old folk material. The Three Bears are friendly bears. They are angry with Goldilocks because she entered their home without permission. The wolf chases Red Riding Hood's grandmother into a closet, instead of devouring her. In the old version of the "Three Billy Goats Gruff" the troll has his eyeballs poked out and is crushed to bits. The modern version has the troll butted into the river and swimming away never to return. The first two

---

[3]Lee, J.: Play in Education. Natural Recreation Assn., N. Y., 1942

little pigs are no longer devoured by the wolf but make an exciting escape to the house of the wise pig.

Any idea that may cause the young child to lie awake at night is best omitted from the program. It is well to discuss make-believe with children. Let them be assured that there are no dragons, really, and that wolves live far away from us. Even such innocent stories as "Little Black Sambo" have caused children to have nightmares with its suggestion of being chased by a tiger.

Another common theme in many of the old tales is the cruelty of step-parents and stepbrothers or sisters. Stereotypes which stigmatize kin, old age or social groups have no place in the story hour.

A discussion before telling some of these questionable stories can take care of these elements. The story of a good stepmother such as Abraham Lincoln's, provides a balance to "Cinderella." There are many good and kind old ladies to balance the one in "Hansel and Gretel."

We should remember that the horror that an adult senses in a story such as "Snow White" is quite different from a child's point of view. Death, and even torture, for many children have only incidental significance. Death is frequently an acceptable solution to a problem. Children play cowboy and Indian, good men and bad men with violent shouts, agonizing deaths and dramatic hardships in one hour and the next listen with rapt attention to a poem of delicate beauty.

Sometimes children themselves will suggest changes in these stories. This frequently happens as they dramatize a story. Another interesting variation of the traditional material is to put the characters in a new situation. Make up a story of visiting the three bears for Christmas or let Cinderella go to school.

Third, a storyteller knows that preparation is needed to make a story vivid to listeners. After a careful reading, put the story aside and think about it until you can picture the story to yourself—clearly in all details. Check any doubts by reading the story again. It is better for a beginning storyteller to know a few stories well than to attempt so many that none can be told with complete confidence. The "tell it again" quality of stories is a great safeguard for beginners. Any storyteller is almost sure to tell a story better each additional time he tells it.

And fourth, a storyteller knows that the audience must be comfortable. The audience must be free from interruptions during the story and it must end before they become weary or bored. Wait a few moments before starting a story so that there is a hush of expectancy in the room. If there are those who are inattentive, pause until quiet is restored. If many grow restless, it is quite obvious that you have the wrong story. Don't blame the children. Just say, "I guess this isn't the right story so let's stand up and stretch." Then go on with some other group activity such as marching, a song, or a fingerplay. Start another story only when there is expectancy and readiness for whole-hearted listening.

These techniques should be used as a story is told with the flannel board.

1. Place the flannel board where it will remain securely in a place that can be seen by all students. The chalk board is good if the group is in a small circle seated before it. An easel is better if the board must be seen by an entire room. If children are seated on a rug, they must be farther away from the teacher than when she uses a picture book. Those in front will be under a strain looking up if they are too near the board.

2. Arrange the figures to be used in the sequence needed for telling the story. It is best to keep them in a folder away from the sight of the listeners. Otherwise, some of the surprise and suspense is lost as they are introduced. A Manila folder used in file cabinets makes a good container. Staple a pocket on one side of the folder to hold the figures and staple the story to the other side.

3. There is a tendency to look away from the listeners to the figures as they are placed on the flannel board. Of course this is necessary. Try to use this movement to direct the listeners' eyes but turn back to the audience as you tell the story. Otherwise, you will find yourself talking to the flannel board, thus creating a hearing problem for your audience.

15

4. Plan your follow-up before you tell the story. Are you going to evaluate the story? Are you going to have the children retell parts of the story? Are you going to have the children create a favorite story? When a story ends in the classroom it is a bit different from the ending of a play in the theater or a television program. The audience is still with you. Instead of going home or turning on another station you must plan the transition to the next school task.

How to Make a Flannel Board

Courtesy of Dr. Francis Ballentine,
Professor of Education, San Diego State College

This board is especially planned to be used in arithmetic as well as language arts. While one side is the conventional flannel board, the other provides a maneuverable drill area in arithmetic by providing a place to manipulate tongue depressors which act as counters.

MATERIALS

    1 piece of plywood ⅜″ x 24″ x 32″.

    1 piece of heavy flannel or coat lining 28″ x 36″.

    3 pieces 1″ quarter round 32″ long.

(This is a strip of wood shaped like this)

    3 pieces ¾″ x 26″ black elastic.

    15 1-inch No. 17 brads.

STEPS

1. Select the better of the two sides of the plywood for place value chart.
2. Starting at base 32 inches long, mark up on each 24-inch edge a mark at 3″, 8″, 11″, 18″ and 19″.

16

3. Make similar marks on reverse side.

4. Staple elastic at 4″, 12″ and 20″ lines. Staple ends on reverse side from place value chart so that the elastic goes over the edge of the board.

5. Cover the poorer of the two sides with heavy flannel. Turn excess flannel over edges to place value side. Turn under the raw edges, miter corners and staple.

6. Fasten quarter round to place value side with brads.
   Place 1 piece at base, 1 piece on top of 8″ mark and 1 piece on top of 18″ mark.

7. Material for use.

   Tongue depressors are used for counters. See the school nurse for best local source.

   Any felt figures.

   Pictures made of construction paper which have been backed with flannel, heavy sandpaper or commercial flocking paper.

   Use rubber cement instead of glue to place the flannel or sandpaper to the figures.

For scenery use light flannel and draw with wax crayons the trees, lakes or castles needed.

Some figures look better if outlined with ink. A number of companies have tubes with a felt point designed for this purpose. They go under trade names such as Magic Marker. A large stationery store will have a supply.

The flannel board is heavier than one made of cardboard, but it is much more durable. If the children make individual boards, cardboard such as the back of tablets, or the cardboard used by laundries to wrap men's shirts, is quite all right. The flannel can be mounted on this with tape rather than staples.

Chapter II

Beginning Stories

Queer Company

FRANCES WICKES
Courtesy Speech Course of Study
Los Angeles City Schools

A little old woman lived all alone in a little old house in the woods.

One Halloween she sat in the chimney corner, and as she sat, she spun.

> Still she sat and
> Still she spun and
> Still she wished for company.

Then she saw her door open a little way, and in came

> A pair of broad, broad feet,
> And sat down by the fireside.
>
> "That is strange," thought the little old
> woman, but—
>
> Still she sat and
>
> Still she spun and
>
> Still she wished for company.

Then in came,

> A pair of long, long legs,
>
> And sat down on the broad, broad feet;
>
> "Now that is strange," thought the old
> woman, but—

Still she sat and

Still she spun and

Still she wished for company.

Then in came,

A wee, wee waist,

And sat down on the long, long legs.

"Now that is strange," thought the old
woman, but—

Still she sat and

Still she spun and

Still she wished for company.

Then in came,

A pair of broad, broad shoulders,

And sat down on the wee, wee, waist.

But—

Still she sat and

Still she spun and

Still she wished for company.

Then in through the door came,

A pair of long, long arms,

And sat down on the broad, broad shoulders.

"Now that is strange," thought the little
old woman, but—

Still she sat and

Still she spun and

Still she wished for company.

Then in came,

A pair of fat, fat hands,

And sat down on the long, long arms.

But—

Still she sat and

Still she spun and

Still she wished for company.

Then in came,

A round, round head,

And sat down on top of all

That sat by the fireside.

The little old woman stopped her spinning and asked,

"Where did you get such big, big feet?"

"By much tramping, by much tramping," said Somebody.

"Where did you get such long, long legs?"

"By much running, by much running," said Somebody.

"Where did you get such a wee, wee waist?"

"Nobody knows, nobody knows," said Somebody.

"Where did you get such broad, broad shoulders?"

"From carrying brooms," said Somebody.

"Where did you get such long, long arms?"

"Swinging the scythe, swinging the scythe," said Somebody.

"Where did you get such fat, fat hands?"

"From threshing, from threshing," said Somebody.

"How did you get such a huge, huge head?"

"Of a pumpkin I made it," said Somebody.

Then said the little old woman, "What did you come for?"

"*YOU!*"

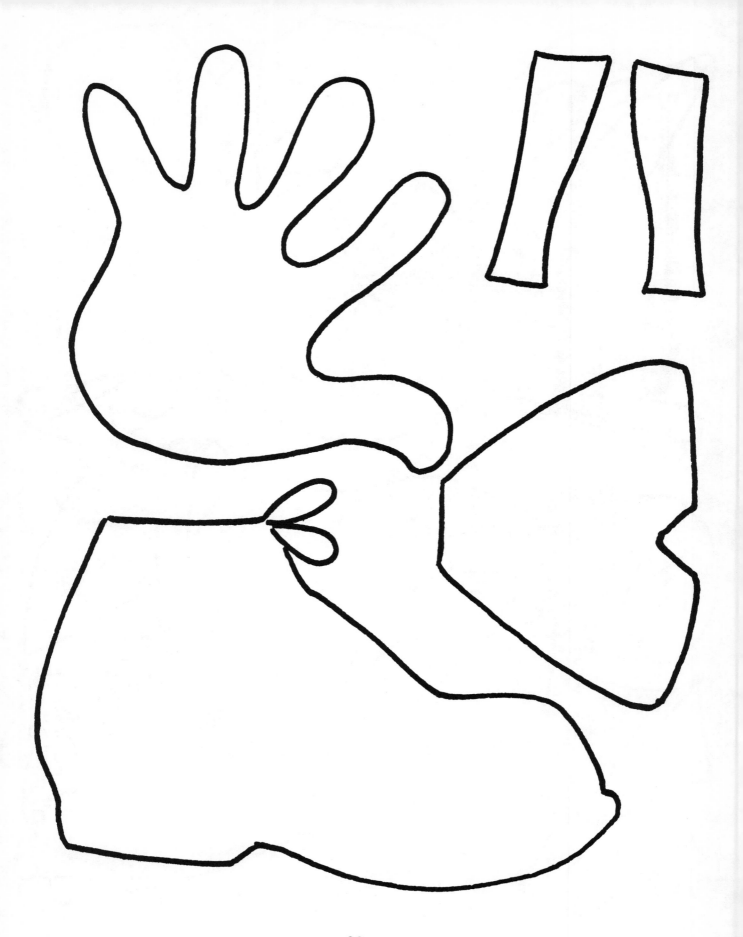

The Teeny Tiny Woman

Old English Tale

There was once a teeny tiny woman who lived in a teeny tiny house in a teeny tiny village. Now one day this teeny tiny woman put on her teeny tiny bonnet and went out to take a teeny tiny walk. When she had gone a teeny tiny way she came to a teeny tiny market. There she saw a teeny tiny bone.

"This teeny tiny bone will make me a teeny tiny soup for my teeny tiny supper," said the teeny tiny woman to her teeny tiny self. So the teeny tiny woman bought the teeny tiny bone and put it into her teeny tiny pocket and went home to her teeny tiny house.

Now when the teeny tiny woman got home to her teeny tiny house, she was a teeny tiny bit tired, so she put the teeny tiny bone in her teeny tiny cupboard and went up her teeny tiny stairs to her teeny tiny bed.

When this teeny tiny woman had been asleep a teeny tiny time, she was awakened by a teeny tiny voice from the teeny tiny cupboard which said: "Give me my bone!"

The teeny tiny woman was a teeny tiny bit frightened, so she hid her teeny tiny head under the teeny tiny bed covers and went to sleep again. And when she had been asleep again a teeny tiny time, the teeny tiny voice cried out from the teeny tiny cupboard a teeny tiny bit louder: "GIVE ME MY BONE!"

This made the teeny tiny woman a teeny tiny bit more frightened, so she hid her teeny tiny head a teeny tiny way farther under the teeny tiny bed covers. And when the teeny tiny woman had been asleep again a teeny tiny time, the teeny tiny voice from the teeny tiny cupboard said again, a teeny tiny bit louder: "GIVE ME MY BONE!"

At this the teeny tiny woman was a teeny tiny bit more frightened, but she put her teeny tiny head out from under the teeny tiny bed covers, and said in her loudest teeny tiny voice: *"TAKE IT!"*

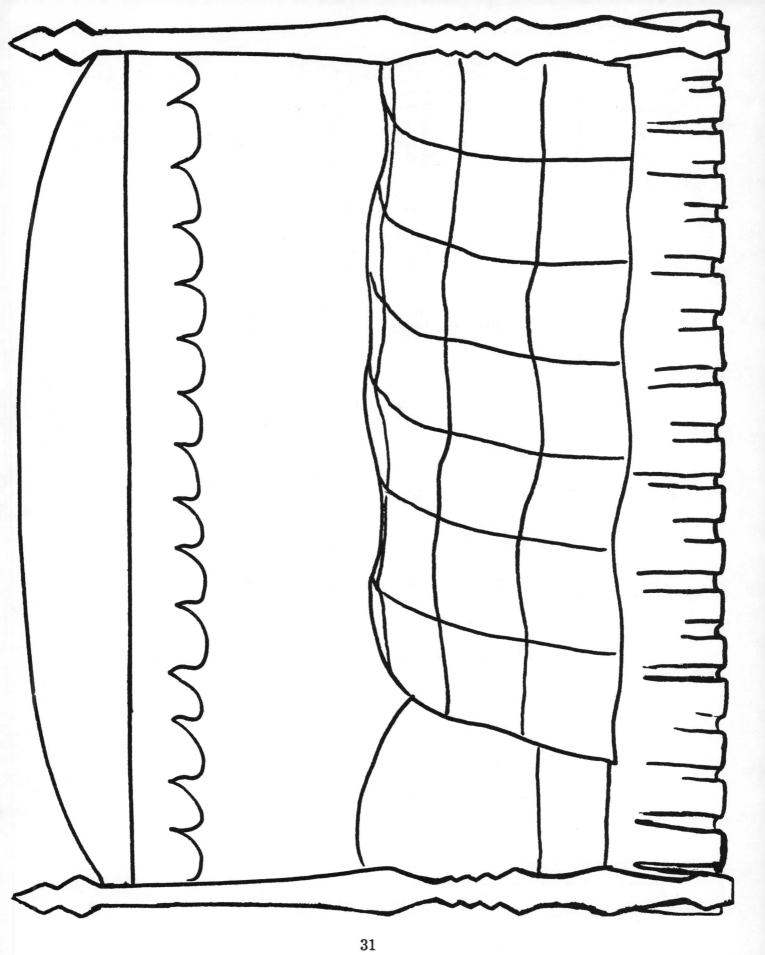

Halloween Subtraction

MARY ALICE KELLY

Three little ghosts on Halloween night,

　　Saw a witch and shrieked in fright.

The witch just laughed and shouted,

　　"Boo!"

One ghost ran home, and that left two.

Two little ghosts in two little sheets

　　Went to a door to say, "Trick or treats."

But when the door swung open wide,

　　A scary goblin stood inside.

One ghost gulped and said to the other,

　　"I'm going home and stay with my mother."

Of the three little ghosts, there was now one alone,

　　Too frightened to utter a groan or a moan.

One little ghost who shivered and shook

With every single step he took,

A fraidy-cat ghost can't have much fun,

So he cried, "Wait for me!" and then

there was none.

The Story of Thanksgiving

San Diego City Schools

Many, many years ago, a small ship came to America. The name of this ship was the *Mayflower*. The people on this ship were called *Pilgrims*. They were among the first to settle our country. (Call attention to the clothing of the period.) The Pilgrims wore different clothing than we do today.

It was very cold when they came to America and they didn't have **very** much food left.

They made friends with the *Indians*. The Indians taught the Pilgrims how to build houses and hunt for food and live in the wilderness.

They were very glad when spring came and it was warm again. They went to work right away. They plowed the land. They planted the seeds they had carried from England across the ocean to America. And then they waited.

All summer the sun shone. The rain watered the plants. The plants grew strong and healthy. When fall came the Pilgrims gathered their *fruits* and *vegetables* they had planted. They stored away enough food for the next winter.

Everyone was very happy and the Pilgrims said, "We must thank God for all the good food, our homes, our clothes, our friends and all our blessings. We will have a big feast and invite our Indian friends. We will call it a feast of Thanksgiving."

On the day of the feast the Pilgrims covered the tables with good things to eat from their gardens. The Indians brought wild turkeys they had shot

37

with their bows and arrows. At that time there were wild turkeys all over America. So you see the turkey is a real American bird. Today farmers raise enough turkeys for our Thanksgiving or any other feast.

Before anyone ate they all bowed their heads. Then they said a prayer of thanksgiving to God. That was the first Thanksgiving. It took place many, many years ago. Now Thanksgiving is a legal holiday and we do not come to school on that day. On Thanksgiving this year remember to thank God for all the good things He has given *you*.

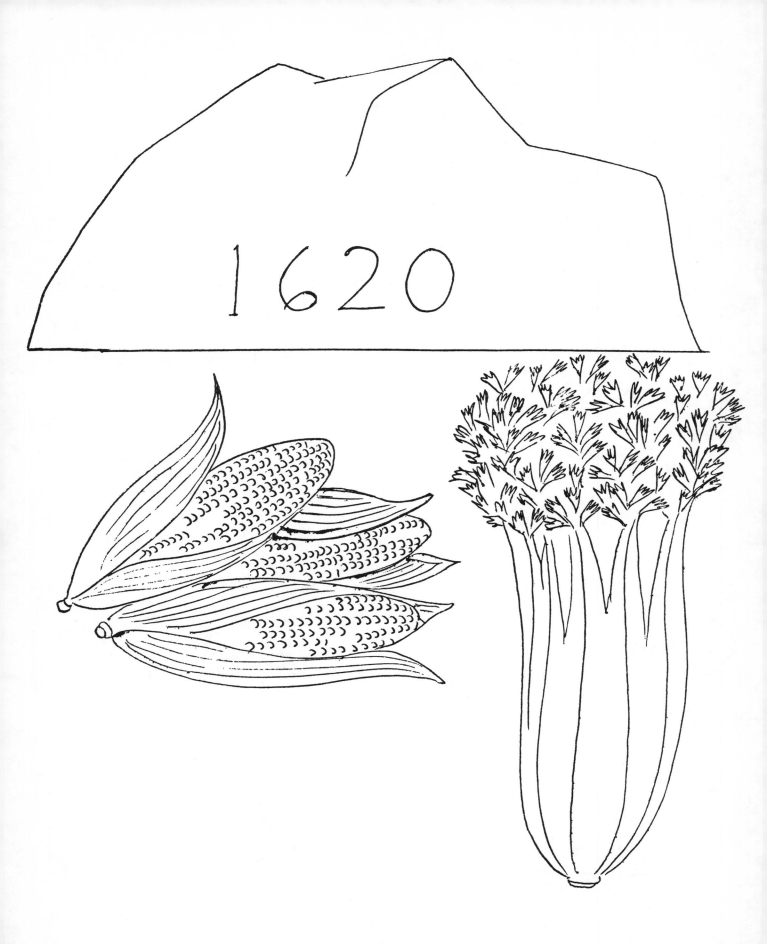

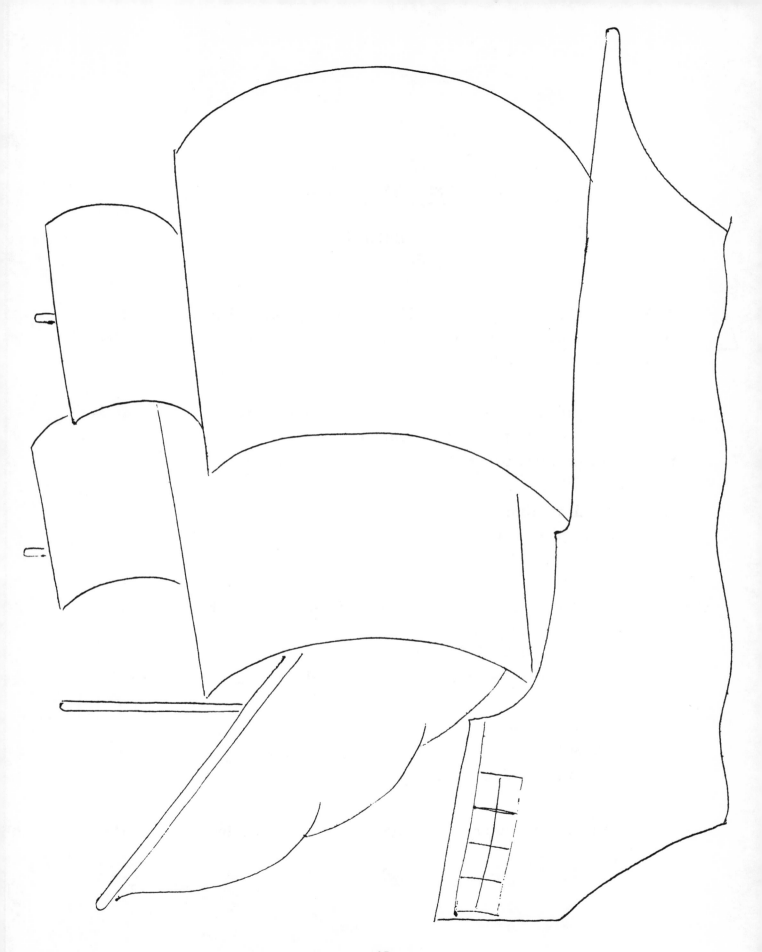

The Big, Big Turnip

Traditional

A farmer once planted a turnip seed. And it grew, and it grew, and it grew. The farmer saw it was time to pull the turnip out of the ground. So he took hold of it and began to pull.

> He pulled and he pulled and he pulled and he pulled
> But the turnip wouldn't come up.

So the farmer called to his wife who was getting dinner.

> Fe, fi, fo, fum
> I pulled the turnip
> But it wouldn't come up.

And the wife came running, and she took hold of the farmer, and they pulled and they pulled and they pulled and they pulled.
But the turnip wouldn't come up.

So the wife called to the daughter who was feeding the chickens nearby.

> Fe, fi, fo, fum
> We pulled the turnip
> But it wouldn't come up.

And the daughter came running. The daughter took hold of the wife. The wife took hold of the farmer. The farmer took hold of the turnip. And they pulled and they pulled and they pulled and they pulled. But the turnip wouldn't come up.

So the daughter called to the dog who was chewing a bone.

Fe, fi, fo, fum
We pulled the turnip
But it wouldn't come up.

And the dog came running. The dog took hold of the daughter. The daughter took hold of the wife. The wife took hold of the farmer. And the farmer took hold of the turnip. And they pulled and they pulled and they pulled and they pulled. But the turnip wouldn't come up.

So the dog called to the cat who was chasing her tail.

Fe, fi, fo, fum
We pulled the turnip
But it wouldn't come up.

And the cat came running. The cat took hold of the dog. The dog took hold of the daughter. The daughter took hold of the wife. The wife took hold of the farmer. The farmer took hold of the turnip. And they pulled and they pulled and they pulled and they pulled. But the turnip wouldn't come up.

So the cat called the mouse who was nibbling spinach nearby.

Fe, fi, fo, fum
We pulled the turnip
But it wouldn't come up.

And the mouse came running.

"That little mouse can't help," said the dog. "He's too little."

"Phooey," squeaked the mouse. "I could pull that turnip up myself, but since you have all been pulling I'll let you help too."

So the mouse took hold of the cat. The cat took hold of the dog. The dog took hold of the daughter. The daughter took hold of the wife. The wife took hold of the farmer. The farmer took hold of the turnip. And they pulled and they pulled and they pulled and they pulled. And *UP* came the turnip.

And the mouse squeaked, "I told you so!"

The Little Dog Who Forgot How to Bark

San Diego City Schools

Kiki was a little black and white dog. He had two black ears. His paws were white. He had a black spot in the middle of his back.

Kiki was very unhappy. He had forgotten how to bark. He tried to think how to bark. He tried and tried.

At last he went to Gray Owl. Gray Owl was very wise. He looked at Kiki. He ruffled up his feathers.

Gray Owl said, "I will tell you how to bark. It is like this: WHOO-whooo-oo!"

"No! No!" said Kiki. "That may be the way a gray owl barks but it is not the way a little dog barks."

Kiki ran to White Duck.

White Duck looked at Kiki. She stretched her neck. Then she said, "I will tell you how to bark. It is like this: Quack, quack, quack!"

"No! No!" said Kiki. "That may be the way a white duck barks but I am sure it is not the way a little dog barks."

Kiki ran to Big Pig.

Big Pig was eating corn. He looked at Kiki. He did not want to stop eating corn. He looked cross.

Big Pig said, "I will tell you how to bark. It is like this: Oink, oink, oink! Now run along and play. I am busy."

"No! No!" said Kiki. "That may be the way a big pig barks but it is not the way a little dog barks."

Kiki ran to Turkey Gobbler. Turkey Gobbler spread his tail. It was a big tail. Turkey Gobbler was proud of it.

He said, "I will tell you how to bark. It is like this: Gobble, gobble, gobble!"

"No! No!" said Kiki. "That may be the way a turkey gobbler barks but that is not the way a little dog barks."

Kiki ran to Red Calf.

Red Calf looked at Kiki and said, "I will tell you how to bark. It is like this: Ma-a-a, m-a-a, m-a-a!"

"No! No!" said Kiki. "That may be the way a red calf barks but it is not the way a little dog barks."

Kiki was tired. He lay down under a tree. He thought and thought. Just then he saw another little dog whose name was Spot. Spot was running after Snowball, the Kitten.

Snowball ran up a tree. Spot jumped around and around under the tree. He said, "Bow-wow, bow-wow!"

Kiki jumped up. He said, "Now I remember how to bark. Bow-wow, bow-wow, bow-wow!"

Spot heard Kiki. He came running. Then away they both ran. Kiki was SO glad he knew how to bark again!

Little Duckling Tries His Voice

From MISS ANNE LANGLEY

Once upon a time fat Little Duckling went on a journey into the wide world. He wandered along the Barnyard Road, and presently he saw Kitty Cat.

"Me-ow!" said Kitty Cat.

"O-o-oh!" cried Little Duckling. "Isn't that a *pretty* sound! I think I'll talk that way!"

But do you suppose Little Duckling could say, "Me-ow"?

No, indeed! He tried, but the best he could do was "Me-e-ack! Me-e-ack!" And that wasn't pretty at all!

So Little Duckling waddled on and on. After a while he saw Puppy Dog.

"Bow-wow!" said Puppy Dog.

"O-o-oh!" cried Little Duckling. "Isn't that a *lovely* noise! I think I'LL talk that way."

But do you suppose Little Duckling could say, "Bow-wow"?

No, indeed! He tried, but this is the way he sounded: "B-ack! B-ack!" And that wasn't lovely at all!

Then Little Duckling waddled on and on. Soon he saw a Yellow Bird in a tree.

"Tweet-tweet-tweet-tweet!" said Yellow Bird.

"Oh, oh, oh!" sighed Little Duckling. "Isn't that a sweet song? I think I'll sing that way!"

But do you suppose Little Duckling could sing, "Tweet-tweet"?

No, indeed! He tried his very best, but all he could say was: "Tw-ack! Tw-ack!" And that wasn't sweet at all!

So Little Duckling waddled on and on. After a while he met Big Cow.

"Moo-o-o!" said Big Cow.

"O-o-oh!", thought Little Duckling. "Isn't that a beautiful roar? I think I'll roar that way!"

But do you suppose Little Duckling could say, "Moo-o-o"?

He tried, but all he could manage to say was: "M-ack! M-ack!" And that wasn't beautiful at all!

Little Duckling was very sad. He could not say "Me-ow" like Kitty Cat. He could not say "Bow-wow" like Puppy Dog. He could not say "Tweet, tweet" like Yellow Bird. He could not say "Moo-o-o" like Big Cow.

He waddled slowly on and on. All at once he saw his own Mother Duck coming toward him along the Barnyard Road.

"Quack! Quack!" cried Mother Duck.

"O-o-oh!" whispered happy Little Duckling to himself. "That is the prettiest sound in the whole wide world! I think I'll talk that way!"

And he found that he could say, "Quack! Quack!" very nicely.

The Runaway Cookies

San Diego County Kindergarten Club

The cookie jar people
Hopped out one night
When the cookie jar lid
Was not on tight.

The gingerbread man
Opened raisin eyes
And looked about
In great surprise.

The frosted bunny
Twinkled his nose
And danced around
On his cookie toes.

The sugary duck
Began to quack
And shake the sugar
Off his back.

The cinnamon bear
Could only grunt
For he was too fat
To do a stunt.

The coconut lamb
Jumped up so high
That his little white tail
Flew toward the sky.

They were all so happy
To be at play
That they danced and danced
And danced away.

They danced away
So very far
That they never came back
To the cookie jar.

Wee Red Shoes

Unknown

Once there were some wee red shoes. They lived in a shoeshop. They lived there a long time. "This is no fun," said one wee red shoe. "I want to run," said the other wee red shoe. So they ran out of the shoeshop. They ran down the street patter, patter, patter. They saw a speckled hen.

"Stop!" called Speckled Hen. "I want to wear you." She jumped into wee red shoes. "Now scratch!" said Speckled Hen. "We cannot scratch," said wee red shoes. "Then I cannot wear you," said Speckled Hen. "Run along!" Wee red shoes ran on. They ran and ran—patter, patter, patter.

They saw Brown Duck. "Stop!" called Brown Duck. "I want to wear you." She jumped into wee red shoes. "Now swim!" said Brown Duck. "We cannot swim," said wee red shoes. "Then I cannot wear you," said Brown Duck. "Run along!" Wee red shoes ran on. They ran and ran—patter, patter, patter.

They saw Dog Nero. "Stop!" called the dog. "I want to wear you." He jumped into wee red shoes. "Now run!" said the dog. "There are only two of us," said wee red shoes. "You need four shoes." "Then I cannot wear you," said the dog. "Run along!" So wee red shoes ran on. They ran and ran—patter, patter, patter.

They saw a wee girl. She was barefoot. She was crying. Wee red shoes jumped on wee red girl. She saw the wee red shoes. She stopped crying.

"Will you wear us?" asked the wee red shoes. "We will run for you."

"Will you run to school?" asked the wee girl.

"Yes," answered the wee red shoes. "We will run to school every day."

"Oh, thank you, thank you!" said the girl. "Now I can go to school."

Then the wee red shoes were happy. The wee girl was happy. Away they all ran to school—patter, patter, patter.

Los Zapatitos Rojos
(Autor Desconocido)
(Traducido por Leila V. Tossas)

Hace mucho tiempo existieron unos zapatitos rojos. Estos zapatitos habían vivido en una tienda de zapatos por mucho tiempo. "Esto no es divertido," dijo uno de los zapatitos rojos. "Yo quiero correr," dijo el otro zapatito rojo. Así pues, salieron corriendo de la tienda. Corrieron calle abajo, zapateando, zapateando, zapateando. Los zapatitos vieron una gallina pinta.

"¡ Alto ahí!" gritó Gallina Pinta. "Yo quiero usarlos a ustedes." De un salto se puso los zapatitos rojos. "Ahora, ¡ a escarbar!" dijo Gallina Pinta. "Nosotros no podemos escarbar," dijeron los zapatitos rojos. "Entonces yo no puedo usarlos a ustedes," dijo Gallina Pinta. "¡ Váyanse de aquí!" Los zapatitos rojos siguieron corriendo. Corrieron y corrieron—zapateando, zapateando, zapateando.

Los zapatitos rojos vieron a Pata Parda. "¡ Alto ahí!" gritó Pata Parda. "Yo quiero usarlos a ustedes." De un salto se puso los zapatitos rojos. "Ahora, ¡ a nadar!" dijo Pata Parda. "Nosotros no podemos nadar," dijeron los zapatitos rojos. "Entonces yo no puedo usarlos a ustedes," dijo Pata Parda. "¡ Váyanse de aquí!" dijo Pata Parda. Los zapatitos rojos siguieron corriendo. Corrieron y corrieron — zapateando, zapateando, zapateando.

Los zapatitos rojos vieron a Perro Nerón. "¡ Alto ahí!" dijo el perro. "Yo quiero usarlos a ustedes." De un salto se puso los zapatitos. "Ahora, ¡ a correr!" dijo el perro. "Solamente somos dos," dijeron los zapatitos rojos. "Tú necesitas cuatro zapatos." "Entonces no puedo usarlos a ustedes," dijo el perro. "Váyanse de aquí." Así pues los zapatitos rojos siguieron corriendo. Ellos corrieron y corrieron,—zapateando, zapateando, zapateando.

Ellos vieron a una niñita. Estaba descalza. La niñita lloraba. Los zapatitos rojos cruzaron de un salto la distancia entre ellos y la niñita. Ella los vió y dejó de llorar. "¿ Nos usarás?" preguntaron los zapatitos rojos. "Correremos por tí." "¿ Correrán a la escuela?" preguntó la niñita. "Sí," contestaron los zapatitos rojos. "Correremos hacia la escuela todos los días." "¡ Oh, gracias, gracias!" dijo ella. "Ahora puedo ir a la escuela."

Entonces los zapatitos rojos fueron felices. La niñita fué feliz. Todos corrieron hacia la escuela—zapateando, zapateando, zapateando.

"The Spanish version of this story was suggested and first used by Mrs. H. Long of the National City Schools. This translation was done by Dr. L. Tossas of San Diego State College."

The Scarecrow

San Diego County Kindergarten Club

Once upon a time a grandmother who lived in the country had a large cherry tree. It was loaded with ripe, red cherries. Now this grandmother was not so spry as she used to be. She could not climb to the top of the tree to pick the red, ripe cherries to put in a pie. She had to wait until her grandson, Jack, came from the city. Jack's father had promised to bring him the next Saturday. But now it was Wednesday.

Grandmother didn't know what to do. She wanted to wait for Jack to pick the cherries, but how could she? Something was taking them and it was the blackbirds. If something was not done about it at once, the cherries would all be gone. So she thought and thought of some way to frighten the birds away. Finally she had an idea. Do you know what she did?

(Have the children make guesses until the scarecrow is suggested
and then develop it on the flannel boards.)

Grandmother took a stick and stuck it in the ground. She hung an old shirt on it. She tied a bundle of straw on it for a head. She tied on some old ragged overalls. She fastened old gloves for hands. When the wind blew it made him flop just like a man, and the birds didn't dare go near to steal any more cherries.

Now, Grandmother's funny old scarecrow could move his head. I'll show you how and you can move your head that way, too.

(MOTIONS: Head relaxed, bob forward, to one side, backward, to other side. Arms may dangle and hands shake as if blown by the wind.)

Finish with this poem:

> The old scarecrow is such a funny man,
>
> He flops in the wind as hard as he can.
>
> He flops to the right,
>
> He flops to the left,
>
> He flops back and forth,
>
> Till he's almost out of breath.
>
> His arms swing out; his legs swing too.
>
> He nods his head in a how-do-you-do.
>
> See him flippity flop when the wind blows hard,
>
> The old scarecrow in our back yard.

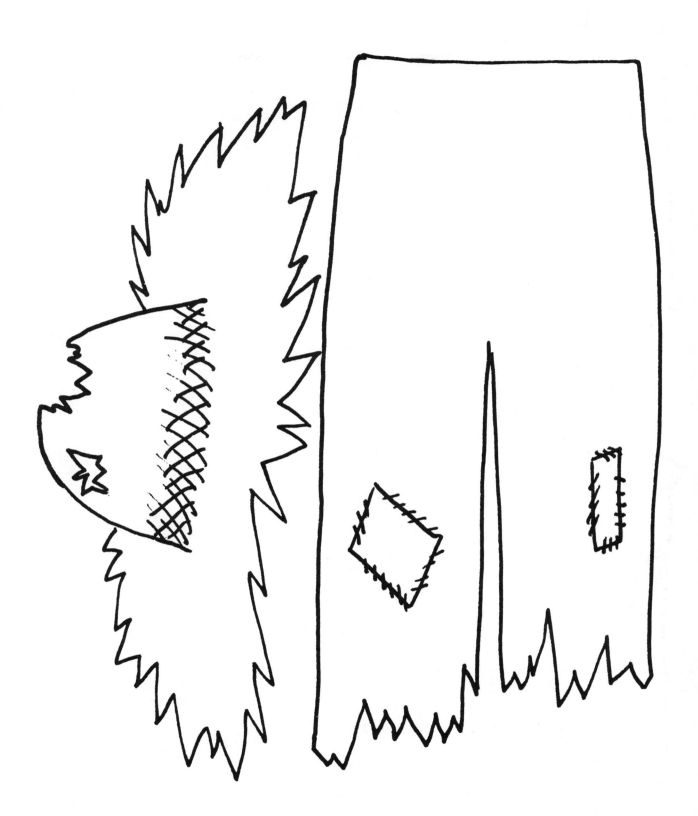

Chapter III

Traditional Stories

The Little Rabbit Who Wanted Red Wings

BY CAROLYN SHERWIN BAILEY*

Once upon a time there was a little White Rabbit with two beautiful pink ears, and two bright red eyes, and four soft little feet. Such a pretty little white rabbit, but he wasn't happy.

Just think, this little White Rabbit would say to his Mummy, "Oh, Mummy, I wish I had a back full of bristles like Mr. Porcupine's."

And when Miss Puddle-Duck went by in her two little red rubbers, the little White Rabbit would say, "Oh, Mummy, I wish I had a pair of red rubbers like Miss Puddle-Duck's."

So he went on wishing and wishing until his Mummy was quite tired out with his wishing. One day Old Mr. Ground Hog heard him wishing.

Old Mr. Ground Hog is very wise indeed, so he said to the little White Rabbit, "Why don't you go down to the Wishing Pond? And if you look in the water at yourself and turn around three times in a circle, you will get your wish."

So the little White Rabbit trotted off, all by himself through the woods, until he came to a little pond of green water lying in a low tree stump, and that was the Wishing Pond. There was a little, little bird, all red, sitting on the edge of the Wishing Pond to get a drink, and as soon as the little White Rabbit saw him he began to wish again.

"Oh, I wish I had a pair of little red wings!" he said. Just then he looked in the Wishing Pond and he saw his little white face. Then he turned around

*Reprinted with the permission of the copyright owners, The Platt & Munk Company, Inc.

three times and something happened. He began to have a queer feeling in his shoulders, like he felt in his mouth when he was cutting teeth. It was his wings coming through. So he sat all day in the woods by the Wishing Pond waiting for them to grow, and by and by when it was almost sundown, he started home to see his Mummy and show her, because he had a beautiful pair of long, trailing red wings.

But by the time he reached home it was getting dark, and when he went to the hole at the foot of the big tree where he lived, his Mummy didn't know him; because, you see, she had never seen a rabbit with red wings in all her life. And so the little White Rabbit had to go out again, because his Mummy wouldn't let him get into his own bed. He had to go out and look for some place to sleep all night.

He went and went until he came to Mr. Bushy Tail's house, and he rapped on the door and said, "Please, kind Mr. Bushy Tail, may I sleep in your house all night?"

But Mr. Bushy Tail opened his door a crack and then he slammed it tight shut again. You see he had never seen a rabbit with red wings in all his life.

So the little White Rabbit went on and on until he came to Miss Puddle-Duck's nest down by the marsh and he said, "Please, kind Miss Puddle-Duck, may I sleep in your nest all night?"

But Miss Puddle-Duck poked her head up out of her nest just a little way and then she shut her eyes and stretched her wings out so far that she covered her whole nest, and said, "No! No! No! Go away!" You see she had never seen a rabbit with red wings in all her life.

So the little White Rabbit went on and on until he came to Old Mr. Ground Hog's hole, and Old Mr. Ground Hog let him sleep with him all night, but the hole had beechnuts spread all over it. Old Mr. Ground Hog liked to sleep on them but they hurt the little White Rabbit and made him very uncomfortable before morning.

When morning came, the little White Rabbit decided to try his wings and fly a little, so he climbed up on a hill and spread his wings and sailed off. But he landed in a low bush all full of prickles, and his four feet got mixed up with twigs so he couldn't get down.

"Mummy! Mummy! Mummy! Come and help me," he called.

His Mummy didn't hear him, but Old Mr. Ground Hog did and came and helped little White Rabbit out of the prickly bush.

"Don't you want your red wings?" Mr. Ground Hog asked.

"No! No!" said the little White Rabbit.

"Well," said the Old Ground Hog, "why don't you go down to the Wishing Pond and wish them off again?"

So the little White Rabbit went down to the Wishing Pond and he saw his face in it. Then he turned around three times and, sure enough, his red wings were gone.

Then he went home to his Mummy, who knew him right away and was so glad to see him. And the little White Rabbit never, never again wished to be something different from what he really was.

The Bear and the Bees

UNKNOWN

Once there was a big brown bear who lived inside a cave with his wife.

"Please, dear," she said to him one day, "run down to the brook and catch some fish for dinner. But don't go near the beehive in the old dead tree. Remember what the bees did to you last time!"

The big brown bear walked slowly toward the brook. Before he knew it, he was at the old dead tree.

As soon as he reached the tree, he pushed his paw into the hive and grabbed a piece of honeycomb. Inside, the busy bees were making wax and honey.

But the minute they saw that big paw wrecking their home and stealing their precious honey, they rushed out.

Swarming after him in a big cloud, the bees were ready to zoom down on his head. So the poor bear had to act fast. Pulling and kicking and tugging, he tore himself loose at last, leaving a great deal of his fur in the brush. He ran toward the brook, jumped into the water, and hid there with only his nose showing. Suddenly the bees spotted him and swooped down smack on his nose.

"Ouch! Ouch!" he cried and ran out of the brook into a grassy field. And he was supposed to catch some fish for dinner!

Back he went to the brook and quickly caught up a trout. Then he ran toward home, looking over his shoulder fearfully.

He was so happy to be home that he gave his wife a great big bear hug and kissed her on both ears. His wife was quite surprised by such a greeting and guessed right away he had done something wrong. And as soon as she saw his nose, she knew what he had done.

She asked him why he went near those bees but he had no excuse. He promised his wife he would never go near that tree again. She gave him the biggest piece of trout and bandaged his nose. But deep down inside he wished the trout would have been some of that nice honey.

Chicken Little

Folk Tale

Once upon a time there was a fluffy chick named Chicken Little. One day as she scratched for food in the orchard, a little apple fell, plop, right on her head. "Oh!" squealed Chicken Little. "What was that? Goodness me!" she cried when she saw the apple. "Oh, the sky has fallen. What shall I do?"

Away ran Chicken Little. She ran so fast she almost bumped into Henny Penny who was just getting off her nest.

"Watch where you are going!" warned Henny Penny. "Why are you running, Chicken Little?"

"Oh, Henny Penny!" cried Chicken Little. "The sky has fallen!"

"How do you know the sky has fallen?" asked Henny Penny.

"I saw it with my eyes," said Chicken Little. "I heard it with my ears. And a piece of it fell on my poor little head."

"How awful," said Henny Penny. "Come, Chicken Little, we must go and tell the king."

They ran until they met Cocky Locky who was strutting along showing off his beautiful feathers. "What's the hurry?" asked Cocky Locky, turning his head so that they could see his fine red comb.

"Oh, Cocky Locky!" said Henny Penny. "The sky has fallen. We are running to tell the king."

"How do you know the sky has fallen?" asked Cocky Locky.

"I saw it with my eyes," said Chicken Little. "I heard it with my ears. And a piece of it fell on my poor little head."

"How terrible!" cried Cocky Locky. "I'll go along with you."

They ran until they saw Ducky Lucky swimming in the pond. "Oh, Ducky Lucky!" called Cocky Locky. "The sky has fallen and we are going to tell the king."

Ducky Lucky waddled out of the water. "How do you know the sky has fallen?" she asked.

"I saw it with my eyes," said Chicken Little. "I heard it with my ears. And a piece of it fell on my poor head."

"Oh, my!" cried Ducky Lucky. "Wait! I'm going with you."

They ran until they met Turkey Lurkey who was spreading his tail into a great big fan. "Can't you stop for a little visit?" asked Turkey Lurkey.

"Not today!" called Ducky Lucky. "The sky has fallen and we must run to tell the king."

"How do you know the sky has fallen?" asked Turkey Lurkey.

"I saw it with my eyes," said Chicken Little. "I heard it with my ears. And a piece of it fell on my poor little head."

"Of course, the king must be told," said Turkey Lurkey. "Follow me and I'll take you to him."

As they ran along they heard a loud, "Hoo—hoo—hoo!" In a tree, Hooty, the owl, blinked his eyes sleepily. "Don't you know this is my nap time?" he scolded. "What is all the noise about?"

What a clucking and quacking there was as each animal told the owl that the sky had fallen.

"Are you sure the sky has fallen?" asked the owl, blinking first one eye, then the other. All the animals looked at Chicken Little as she stepped nearer to the owl.

"A piece of the sky fell on my poor little head. See?" she said as she held her head for him to look.

"Hm-mmm!" said the owl. "Can you show me the piece of sky that fell, Chicken Little?"

"Oh, yes!" said Chicken Little. "Come with me and I'll show you." Chicken Little led the way. The owl flew above her and the animals followed in a line.

When they came to the orchard, Chicken Little said, "Look! There is the piece of sky that fell on my poor little head." All of the animals looked at the little apple. Then, one by one, they walked away—all but the owl. The wise owl looked at Chicken Little.

"That is a little apple from the apple tree," he said. "And if you are a smart little chicken you'll eat it before the others come back to get it."

And that is just what Chicken Little did. She pecked and pecked at it until it was all gone.

The Pancake Man

Norse Folk Story

There was a little old woman, and a little old man. One day the old woman had a pancake in a little old pan. She went to the door and said, "Come, Little Old Man, and look in this pan." The little old man looked in the little old pan and said, "I see just what I want for my dinner. I am going to eat that pancake."

The pancake jumped away from the little old man. He jumped out of the pan to the floor. He rolled over the floor to the door. Then out the door he went in a hurry!

"Stop, Pancake!" said the old man. "Come back to this little old pan!"

The pancake did not stop. He rolled out of the gate and called back, "Run, run, as fast as you can. You cannot catch me. I am the Pancake Man."

The old woman and the old man ran after the pancake, but they could not catch him.

Pancake rolled on and on. Soon he met a big black dog.

"Stop, Pancake!" said the dog. Pancake did not stop. He rolled on and sang, "I ran away from a little old woman and a little old man and I can run away from you too. I am the Pancake Man!"

Pancake rolled on and on. Soon he met a big brown bear.

"Stop, Pancake!" said the bear. Pancake rolled on and he sang, "I ran away from a little old woman and a little old man. I ran away from a big black dog, and I can run away from you too. I am the Pancake Man!"

On rolled the pancake. Next he met a fox. "Good day, Pancake," said the fox. "Did I hear you sing as you rolled down the hill? Come here and sing for me."

The Pancake Man sang, "I ran away from a little old woman and a little old man. I ran away from a big black dog and a big brown bear. I can run away from you too. I am the Pancake Man!"

"My, my!" said the fox. "I do not want to run after you. Stay here and sing for me again."

The pancake sat next to the fox and sang, "I ran away from a little old woman and a little old man. I ran away from a big black dog and a big brown bear. I can run away from you too. I am the Pancake Man!"

"You will never run away again," said the fox. "You are just what I want for my dinner. I am going to eat you up!" And that is just what he did!

The Three Wishes

Folk Tale

Once, many years ago, there was a poor woodcutter and his wife who lived from day to day in a humble cottage near the edge of the woods. Every day the man would go into the forest to chop wood and return in time for supper. Then, they usually talked about the good things that their neighbors owned, and wished that they, too, might have such good things.

One day, while the woodcutter was in the forest, he said aloud, as he had often said before, "Oh, it is a hard life! I have to work so hard all day long, and yet I am still poor. There are so many things I would like to have —if only I could ever hope to get them!"

As he uttered these words a beautiful fairy appeared before him. "I have heard your complaints," she said, "and so, I shall grant you three wishes. Choose them wisely, because you may have no more than three." Then she faded from view as mysteriously as she had appeared.

When the woodcutter went home that evening, he told his wife what had happened, and they were both so excited they could hardly eat. "Imagine!" said the wife. "We can ask for anything we like—anything! Oh, I'm so happy!"

"Yes, it is wonderful," agreed the man. "Just think—we can have great wealth!"

"Or a fine house," said his wife.

"Even a mansion—or a palace," added the husband, his eyes shining brightly.

They went on talking in this way, thinking of all the things they could possibly wish for, but they could not agree on any one wish right away, so they decided to put it off until the next day. Then they sat down to the table to eat.

The man looked at the bowl of soup that was before him and sighed. "Oh, dear, soup again!" he said. "How I wish for once that I could have a nice fat sausage!"

Wonder of wonders, at that very instant, a plump sausage appeared magically on the table!

The wife was the first to realize what had happened. "Now look what you have done!" she cried. "You have wasted a wish on a silly old sausage. Now we have only two wishes left!"

"Oh, well, there is still much to be wished for," said the man.

"Is that all you have to say for yourself?" scolded the woman. "Here you have wasted a perfectly good wish for all time. How could you have been so foolish?" And she went on like that, complaining loudly.

Soon the man lost his patience and exclaimed, "I am tired of hearing about the sausage! I am tired of hearing you speak! I wish that the sausage were stuck to your nose!"

No sooner were the words out of his mouth than the sausage was hanging at the end of his wife's nose!

"Now see what you have done!" cried the wife. "You have wasted another wish by your foolish tongue!" And she tried desperately to remove the sausage from the end of her nose, but it would not come off.

"We still have one wish left," said the husband. "We can still wish for great wealth."

"What good is money or riches," the woman asked, "if I must go through life with a sausage on the end of my nose? Everyone would laugh at me and I could not abide that! No, there is only one thing to do, and that is to wish it off."

"But then we will be left as poor as we were before," said the husband.

"That is all that I wish for," said the wife. And in a flash, the sausage was gone.

The three wishes had been granted, and for all of their plans, the woodcutter and his wife were no better off. In fact, sad to say, they could not even have sausage for dinner.

The Steadfast Tin Soldier

BY HANS CHRISTIAN ANDERSEN

There were once five-and-twenty tin soldiers who were all brothers, for they were all born of one old tin spoon. They all carried guns and stood eyes front. Their beautiful uniforms were red and blue. The very first thing they heard in this world when the lid was taken off the box they lay in, were the words, "Tin Soldiers!" It was a little boy who shouted it and clapped his hands. He had been given them because it was his birthday, and now he set them up on the table.

Each soldier was exactly like his neighbor. There was only one who was a little different. He had one leg. He had been the last one to be cast and there was not enough tin left. Still, he stood just as steady on his one leg as the rest did on their two, and it is he to whom we have to pay attention.

On the table where they were set up stood a great many other toys, but the one which caught the eye the most was a lovely paper castle. Through the little windows you could see right into the room. In front of it, little trees stood around a tiny looking glass, which was meant to look like a lake. Swans made of wax swam on it and looked at their reflections. The whole thing was very pretty, but prettiest of all was a little Lady who stood in the open door of the castle. She too was cut out of paper, but she had a skirt of the finest possible muslin, and a little painted blue stripe crossing her shoulder like a scarf. In the middle of it was a bright spangle as big as the whole of her face. The little Lady had her arms stretched out, for she was a dancer, and one of her legs was lifted so high that the Tin Soldier could not see it. He thought that she had only one leg like him.

100

"That would be the wife for me," he thought, "but she's very grand. She lives in a castle, and I have only a box. And there's five-and-twenty of us to go into it. It's no place for her. Still, I must try to get introduced."

Then he laid himself down at his full length behind a snuff box which was on the table. From there he could look straight at the elegant little Lady, who continued to stand on one leg without losing her balance.

In the evening, all the other Tin Soldiers were put into their box, and the people of the house went to bed. Then the toys began to play. They played at "paying calls," at "fighting battles," and "giving balls." The Tin Soldiers rattled in their box, for they wanted to join in, but they could not lift the lid. The Nutcracker turned head-over-heels, the Slate Pencils made a great to-do on the slate. There was such a fuss that the canary woke up and began to speak—in verse! The only two who did not leave their places were the Tin Soldier and the little Lady. She stood straight up on tiptoe, with her arms stretched out; and he was just as steady on his one leg. He did not take his eyes off her for a second. Then the clock struck twelve, and "crack," up sprang the lid of the snuff box. But there was no snuff in it, no, but a little black Goblin; you see, it was just a trick.

"Tin Soldier," said the Goblin, "will you keep your eyes to yourself?"

But the Tin Soldier pretended not to hear.

"Just you wait till tomorrow!" said the Goblin.

Well, when tomorrow came and the children got up, the Tin Soldier was put in the window, and whether it was the Goblin's doing or the draft, all at once the window flew open and the soldier fell down on his head from the third story. It was a terrible fall. His leg pointed straight up, and there he stayed on his cap, with his bayonet stuck between two paving stones.

The maid and the little boy ran down at once to look for him, but though they almost stepped on him, they could not see him. If the Tin Soldier had only shouted, "Here I am!" they would have found him easily enough, but he did not think it proper to call out loudly, because he was in uniform.

It began to rain. The drops came faster, one after another, and it turned into a regular downpour. When it was over, two street boys came running along.

"Just look!" said one of them, "there's a Tin Soldier. He shall go for a voyage."

So they made a boat out of newspaper, put the Tin Soldier in it, and off he sailed, down the gutter. The two boys ran along with him and clapped their hands. Mercy! What waves raged in that gutter and what a stream there was! There had, indeed, been a heavy rain. The paper boat tossed up and down and sometimes spun completely around so that the Tin Soldier became dizzy; but he was as steady as ever and looked straight in front of him, shouldering his gun.

All at once the boat darted under a broad culvert. It was as dark there as it had been in the box.

"Where am I going now?" he thought. "Yes, this is the Goblin's doing. Oh, dear! If that little Lady were here in the boat, I wouldn't care if it were twice as dark!" Suddenly there came a big water rat who lived under the culvert.

"Have you got a pass?" said the rat. "Show me your pass!"

But the stream ran stronger and stronger. The Tin Soldier could see daylight ahead where the culvert ended. But at the same time he heard a rushing sound that was enough to frighten the bravest heart. Think of it! At the end of the culvert the gutter ran straight into a huge canal. For him it was as dreadful as for us to go down a great waterfall in a boat.

Now he was already so near it that he could not stop. On went the boat, and the poor Tin Soldier held himself as still as he could and no one could say that he winked an eye. The boat spun around three or four times, and filled with water to the gunwale—it was bound to sink! The Tin Soldier was up to his neck in water. Deeper and deeper sank the boat. Softer and softer grew the paper.

The water closed over the Soldier's head, and he thought of the pretty little Lady whom he should never see again, and in his ears rang the words:

"Onward, onward, warrior,

Death waits for thee!"

Then the paper parted and the Tin Soldier fell through; but at that moment he was swallowed by a big fish.

Oh, how dark it was in there! It was darker than the culvert, and besides, the space was very narrow. But the Tin Soldier was steady as ever and lay all his length shouldering his gun.

The fish darted here and there and executed the most alarming movements. Finally it became very quiet, then a ray of light seemed to break through. The light shone brightly, and somebody called out: "A TIN SOLDIER!"

The fact was, the fish had been caught, taken to market, sold and taken into the kitchen where a maid cut it open with a big knife. She took the Tin Soldier by the body with both her hands and carried him into the parlor, where everybody wanted to see the remarkable man who had traveled about in the inside of a fish.

They set him up on the table, and there—well! It is funny how things do come about in the world! The Tin Soldier was in the very same room as before! He saw the very same children, and the same toys were on the table; the lovely castle with the pretty little Lady. She was still standing on one leg, with the other lifted high up. She was faithful, too. The Tin Soldier was touched. He was close to tears, but it would not be becoming for a soldier to cry. He looked at her and she looked at him, but neither of them said a word.

At that moment one of the little boys picked up the Tin Soldier and threw him into the stove. He had no explanation to give. It must be the Goblin in the snuff box that was responsible.

The Tin Soldier stood there, all lit up, and felt an overpowering heat. But whether it came from the fire, or from love, he did not know. The colors had all come off him. No one could say whether that had happened on his journey or had been caused by sorrow. He looked at the little Lady, and she looked at him, and he felt that he was melting, but still he stood steady with his gun. Then suddenly the door opened, the wind caught the Dancer, and she flew into the stove to the Tin Soldier. She blazed into flame and then was gone! The Tin Soldier melted down into a lump, and when the maid took out the ashes the next day, she found him in the shape of a little tin heart. But the little Lady—only the spangle was left, and that was a black spot in the center of the little tin heart.

SNUFF

Make from newspaper.

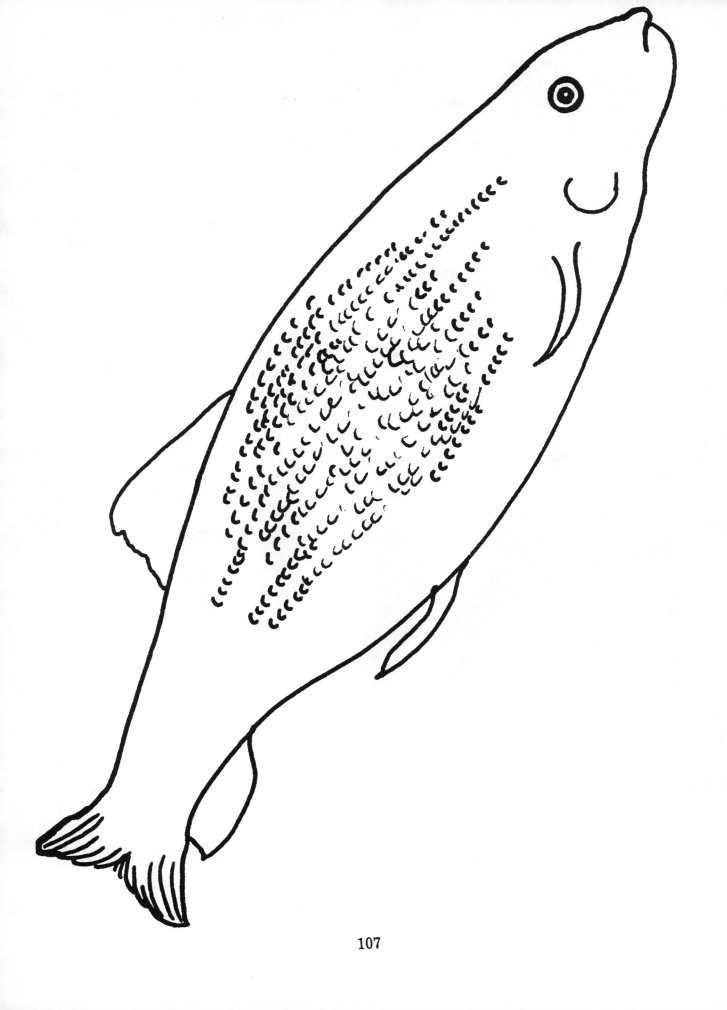

Make 1 amber and 1 yellow
Off-set amber on yellow ¼ inch.
Make dark sections red-orange.

The Emperor's New Clothes

BY HANS CHRISTIAN ANDERSEN

Many years ago there lived an Emperor who was very fond of beautiful new clothes. He spent all his money on them. He did not care about his people or his soldiers. He only liked to drive around and show off his new clothes. He had a coat for every hour of the day.

In the big city where he lived it was always very merry; every day many people visited the city. One day two men came who were really not honest men, but pretended to be weavers. They announced that they could weave the finest materials in the world. Not only were their colors and patterns the finest, but the clothes made from them became invisible to anyone who was unfit for the job he held, or was stupid.

"Those would be extraordinary clothes!" thought the Emperor. "If I wore those, I could tell which men in my kingdom were not fit for their places. I could tell the smart ones from the stupid ones. Yes, the clothes must be made for me at once!"

And he gave the two men a lot of money and told them to begin weaving immediately.

As for them, they put up two looms, and pretended to be working; but they had nothing at all on the looms. They asked for the finest silk and gold; they put this in their own pockets and worked at the empty looms till late into the night.

"I should like to know how far they have gone," thought the Emperor. But he felt uncomfortable when he thought that those who were not fit for their offices could not see it. He believed, indeed, that he had nothing to fear for himself, but he decided to send someone else first. Everyone knew how strange the material was and they were anxious to see how bad or stupid their neighbors were.

"I will send my honest old Minister to the weavers," thought the Emperor. "He can judge best how it looks, for he is wise, and no one knows his office better than he."

Now the Minister went to the hall where the weavers sat working at the empty looms.

"Mercy!" thought the old Minister, and he opened his eyes wide. "I can't see anything at all!" But he did not say this.

The two men begged him to come nearer, and asked if he liked the colors and the pattern. But he could see nothing, for there was nothing to see.

"Mercy!" he thought, "can I be so stupid? None must know. It will never do for me to tell that I could not see the cloth."

"What do you think?" asked one of the weavers.

"It is beautiful," answered the old Minister, as he looked over his glasses. "What a fine color and pattern! Yes, I shall tell the Emperor I am very happy with it."

"Well, we are glad of that," they said. They explained the strange pattern and the Minister listened so that he could tell everything to the Emperor. And he did so.

Now the men asked for more money, silk, and gold, which they said was needed for weaving. This went into their own pockets, and not a thread was put on the frames. They continued to work at the empty looms as before.

The Emperor soon sent another honest Officer to see how the men were doing and how soon the cloth would be ready. He looked and looked but, as there was nothing to see, he could see nothing.

"Isn't this pretty?" asked the weavers; and they went on to explain the lovely pattern which was not there at all.

"I am not stupid!" thought the man. And so he praised the cloth which he could not see. "Yes, it is beautiful," he told the Emperor.

All the people in town were talking about the beautiful cloth. The Emperor wanted to see it himself. With a whole crowd of his friends, including the Minister and the honest Officer, he went to the weaving room. They were weaving very hard but not a thread could be seen.

"Isn't this beautiful?" said the Minister and the Officer. "Does your Majesty like the pattern and colors?" And they pointed to the empty looms, for they thought the others could see the cloth.

"What's this?" thought the Emperor. "I see nothing at all! This is terrible! Am I stupid? Am I not fit to be the Emperor? That would be the most terrible thing that could happen to me. Oh, it is very pretty!" he said aloud. And he looked happy and walked about the empty room, for he would not say that he could see nothing. The men with him looked and looked and saw nothing, but, like the Emperor they said, "That IS pretty!" and begged him to wear the lovely clothes at the great parade soon to take place. "Excellent!" they all cried.

The night before the parade, the two men worked, and kept sixteen candles burning. The people could see that they were hard at work. The two men pretended to take the cloth down from the frames; they made cuts in the air with scissors; they sewed with needles without thread; and at last they said, "The clothes are ready!"

The Emperor came with his soldiers. The two men lifted up one arm as if they were holding something, and said, "See, here are the trousers! Here is the coat! Here is the cloak!" One said, "It is as light as a spider's web. One would think one had nothing on. But that is the wonder of it."

"Yes," said all the soldiers. But they could see nothing.

"Will your Imperial Majesty take off your clothes so that we can put on your new clothes in front of this big mirror?" they asked.

The Emperor took off his clothes and the men pretended to put on his new outfit. He turned round and round in front of the mirror.

"Oh, how nice they look. And what a fit!" said everyone. "What beautiful colors and such a lovely pattern! That IS a wonderful outfit."

The Emperor took a last look in the mirror. "Now I am ready!"

Two servants, who were to carry his train, stooped down with their hands toward the door, just as if they were lifting his cloak; then they pretended to carry it. They did not dare let it be noticed that they saw nothing.

So the Emperor went into the parade, and all the people said, "How beautiful the Emperor's clothes are! What a wonderful cloak! And how perfectly it fits him!" No one would dare say that he could see nothing, for that would show how stupid he was.

"But he has nothing on!" cried a little boy.

Soon others began to say, "But he has nothing on!" This made the Emperor very sad for he knew that they were right. He felt very foolish but he thought to himself, "I must finish the parade." And so he lifted his head higher, the servants held the cloak tighter, and he went on in the clothes which did not exist at all.

(Another story by Hans Christian Andersen that is effective with the flannel board is *The Real Princess.)*

Make two chamberlains

Make throng of people of gray or brown.

117

The Bremen Town Musicians

(A Grimm Fairy Tale)

An honest farmer had once an ancient donkey that had been a faithful servant to him a great many years. But now, however, he was growing old and every day more and more unfit for work. His master therefore was tired of keeping him and began to think of putting an end to him; but the donkey who saw that some mischief was in the wind, took himself slyly off, and began his journey toward the great city, "For there," thought he, "I may turn musician."

After he had traveled a little way he spied a dog lying by the roadside and panting as if he were very tired. "What makes you pant so, my friend?" said the donkey. "Alas!" said the dog, "my master was going to knock me on the head because I am old and weak and can no longer make myself useful to him in hunting; so I ran away. But what can I do to earn my livelihood now?" "Well," said the donkey "I am going to the great city of Bremen to turn musician. Suppose you go with me and try what you can do in the same way!" The dog said he was willing, and they jogged on together.

They had not gone far before they saw a cat sitting in the middle of the road and making a mighty rueful face. "Pray, my good lady," said the donkey, "what's the matter with you? You look quite out of spirit!" "Ah, me!" said the cat, "How can one be in good spirits when one's life is in danger? Because I am beginning to grow old and had rather lie at my ease by the fire than run about the house after the mice, my mistress laid hold of me, and was going to drown me; and though I have been lucky enough to get away from her, I do not know what I am to live upon." "Oh!" said the donkey, "By all means go with us to the great city of Bremen. You are a good night singer, and may make your fortune as a musician." The cat was pleased with the thought, and joined the party.

Soon afterward, as they were passing by a farmyard, they saw a cock perched upon a gate, and screaming out with all his might and main. "Bravo!" said the donkey. "Upon my word, you make a famous noise. Pray what is this all about?" "Why," said the cock, "I was just now saying that we should have fine weather for our washing day, and yet my mistress and the cook don't thank me for my pains, but threaten to cut off my head tomorrow, and make broth of me for the guests that are coming on Sunday!" "Heaven forbid!" said the donkey. "Come with us, Master Chanticleer; it will be better, at any rate, than staying here to have your head cut off! Besides, who knows? If we care to sing in tune, we may get up some kind of a concert; so come along with us." "With all my heart," said the cock. So they all four went on jollily together.

They could not, however, reach the great city the first day, so when night came on, they went into a wood to sleep. The ancient donkey and the good old dog laid themselves down under a great tree, and the cat climbed up into the branches; while the cock, thinking that the higher he sat the safer he should be, flew up into the very top of the tree, and then, according to his custom, before he went to sleep, looked out on all sides of him to see that everything was well. In doing this, he saw afar off something bright and shining, and, calling to his companions, said, "There must be a house no great way off, for I see a light." "If that be the case," said the donkey, "we had better change our quarters, for our lodging is not the best in the world!" "Besides," added the good old dog, "I should not be the worse for a bone or two, or a bit of meat." So they walked off together toward the spot where Chanticleer had seen the light; and as they drew near it became larger and brighter, till they at last came close to a house in which a gang of robbers lived.

The donkey, being the tallest of the company, marched up to the window and peeped in. "Well, donkey," said Chanticleer, "what do you see?" "Why, I see a table spread with all kinds of good things, and robbers sitting round it making merry." "That would be a noble lodging for us," said the cock. "Yes," said the donkey, "if we could only get in." So they consulted together how they could contrive to get the robbers out and at last they hit upon a plan. The donkey placed himself upright on his hind legs, with his forefeet resting against the window; the good old dog got upon his back; the cat scrambled up to the dog's shoulders, and the cock flew up and stuck upon the cat's head. When all was ready, a signal was given and they began their music. The donkey brayed, the dog barked, the cat mewed, and the cock crowed, and then they all broke through the window at once and came tumbling into the room, amongst the glass with a most hideous clatter! The robbers, who had been not a little frightened by the opening concert, had now no doubt that some frightful hobgoblin had broken in upon them, and scampered away as fast as they could.

The coast once clear, our travelers soon sat down and despatched what the robbers had left, with as much eagerness as if they had not expected to eat again for a month. As soon as they had satisfied themselves, they put out the lights, and each once more sought out a resting place to his own liking. The donkey stretched himself upon a mat behind the door; the cat rolled herself up on the hearth before the warm ashes; and the cock perched upon a beam on the top of the house; and the dog curled up in the corner on a pile of old rags; and as they were all rather tired from their journey, they soon fell asleep.

But about midnight, when the robbers saw from afar that the lights were out and that all seemed quiet, they began to think that they had been in too great a hurry to run away; and one of them, who was bolder than the rest, went to see what was going on.

Finding everything still, he marched into the kitchen and groped about till he found a match in order to light a candle; and then, espying the glittering fiery eyes of the cat, he mistook them for live coals, and held the match to them to light it. But the cat, not understanding this joke, sprung at his face, and spit and scratched at him. This frightened him decidedly and away he ran to the nearest door; but there the dog jumped up and bit him in the leg; and as he was crossing over the yard the donkey ran out to him and kicked him; and the cock, who had been awakened by the noise, crowed with all his might.

At this the robber ran very fast back to his comrades and told the captain "how a horrid witch had got into the house, and had spit at him and scratched his face with her long bony fingers; how a man with a knife in his hand had hidden himself behind the door and stabbed him in the leg; how a black monster stood in the yard and struck him with his club, and how the devil had stood upon the top of the house and cried out, 'Throw the rascal up here!' "

After this the robbers never dared to go back to the house; but the musicians were so pleased with their quarters that they took up their abode there; and there they are, I dare say, at this very time.

124

Chapter IV

Modern Stories

Mrs. Peter Pig

BY MABEL WATTS*

Once upon a time there lived some busy, peace-loving friends in a little barnyard town.

There was Mrs. Pecky the Hen, Cock-A-Doo the Rooster, Moo the Cow, Cutie the Kitten, and Gray the Squirrel.

In this same little barnyard town there lived a little pig, whom everybody called Mrs. Peter.

Now Mrs. Peter was a lazy little pig. Although her breakfast dishes were not washed, her beds were not made and her washing was not even started, she decided early one Monday morning to take a walk and visit all her friends in the barnyard town.

All dressed in her nicest clothes, she started out to visit.

She had not gone very far when she met Mrs. Pecky the Hen. She was hanging out her wash.

"Oh, good morning, Mrs. Pecky," said Mrs. Peter. "It's too bad you have to work so hard this nice bright sunny day. Can't you come and take a walk with me? You can do your washing some other nice sunny day."

"Oh, no!" said Mrs. Pecky. "I cannot take a walk until all my washing is done. Besides, it might rain tomorrow, you know. Don't you just love to see a nice line full of clean clothes blowing in the breeze?"

"No, indeed," smiled Mrs. Peter. "I'm not the least bit interested. Besides, I haven't the time." And with that she quickly turned and walked away.

*Reprinted from "Read-Aloud Kindergarten Stories" with permission of the author and Wonder Books, Inc., © 1957.

She had not gone very far, however, before she met Cock-A-Doo the Rooster. He was very busy mowing his lawn.

"Oh, good morning, Cock-A-Doo," said Mrs. Peter. "It's too bad you have to work this nice sunny day. Wouldn't you like to come and take a walk with me? You can mow your lawn tomorrow, you know."

"Oh, no!" said Cock-A-Doo. "I cannot take a walk with you until my lawn is all mowed. You see, it might rain tomorrow. Besides, I do like to see a nice tidy, well-kept lawn, don't you?"

Mrs. Peter shrugged her shoulders and laughed. "I really don't have time to mow my lawn. Besides, it's such hard work." And off she went.

As she turned the corner of the barnyard town, she saw Moo the Cow resting in the grass and chewing her cud.

"Ah!" said Mrs. Peter, half aloud, "I know now who will take a nice stroll with me. Good morning, Moo. Isn't it a nice sunny day? You seem to have nothing at all to do. Come along with me and take a nice walk."

"Humph! Nothing to do, did I hear you say? Well, I am indeed very busy right now, for if all of the children are to have nice rich milk tomorrow, I must rest here in peace and quiet while I chew my cud. Don't you have any shopping to do or any cakes or bread to bake?"

"Oh, no!" said Mrs. Peter. "I don't have time to shop and it's too hot to bake today." And off she went down the road.

When Mrs. Peter asked Cutie the Kitten to walk with her, Cutie replied, "I have a dozen little mittens to wash and tomorrow it may rain all day long."

Now Mrs. Peter was feeling sad. There was only one more neighbor left. Surely Gray the Squirrel would take a walk with her. Just then she looked up and saw Gray dashing across the road. His cheeks were filled with acorns and he was very busy gathering in his winter food supply.

"Won't you take a walk with me?" asked Mrs. Peter sadly.

"Oh, no!" said Gray. "If I do not store away my acorns now, my family will have nothing to eat next winter."

Mrs. Peter frowned. She was really very sad now, for Gray had not even waited for her reply.

Everybody in the barnyard town was too busy to take a walk. Mrs. Pecky the Hen was washing; Cock-A-Doo the Rooster was mowing his lawn; Moo the Cow was chewing her cud; Cutie the Kitten was washing mittens, and Gray the Squirrel was gathering acorns for his family.

It wasn't much fun taking a walk alone. So Mrs. Peter returned home. She put on her white apron and started to work.

She washed her dishes, ironed her clothes, shopped and baked. That evening she was tired, but very happy.

As she sat down to rest, she called all of her little piggies around her. "It must be true," she whispered, "that busy people are always the happiest people."

Wee Ann

by Leila Kendall Browne*

Emily Ann MacMillan Smith was five years old.

But she was so very small that no one ever called her Emily Ann Mac-Millan Smith.

She was so small that Wee Ann fitted her much better.

In fact, she was so small that people had a hard time finding her.

And Wee Ann didn't like that at all.

"Where is Wee Ann?" her mother would ask. "There are cookies and milk for her on the kitchen table."

"Where is Wee Ann?" her father would ask. "It's time to play piggyback to bed."

And Wee Ann was right there all the time.

At school it was especially hard.

Sometimes the children didn't give her a turn at games because they overlooked her.

And this made Wee Ann very sad.

Every day she s-t-r-e-t-c-h-e-d as hard as she possibly could.

Every day she answered "Here I am!" as loudly as was polite, when the teacher called the roll.

But nothing seemed to make much difference, and people still asked where she was.

*Reprinted with permission from *Child Life Magazine*, copyrighted, 1954.

"Don't worry, Wee Ann," everybody said to her. "Sometimes growing tall takes quite a long time to happen."

But that didn't help, because Wee Ann wanted people to see her right now, when she was five years old, without having to take a second look.

One day Wee Ann looked at the calendar, and it was just a month before Christmas. That meant something special. That meant it was time for Wee Ann to write a letter to her Grandmother MacMillan.

And it had to be a very special letter, for Grandmother MacMillan was a very special person. She was very special to Wee Ann.

Grandmother MacMillan lived far across the ocean in a country called Scotland, and Wee Ann had never seen her.

Wee Ann couldn't write all by herself, so she sat down and told her mother exactly what she wanted to say. That way Wee Ann and Grandmother MacMillan wrote lots of letters back and forth across the sea, and they knew all about each other.

Someday Wee Ann was going to Scotland for a visit. She knew all about it, for Grandmother MacMillan had told her about the highlands, and the little streams, called burns, and the old castles, and the wee churches, called kirks, and the big cities.

But of course Wee Ann couldn't go to Scotland if nobody could find her without looking twice, and Grandmother MacMillan didn't know about that.

So Wee Ann decided to tell her.

And she told her about the very worst worry of all. It was just a month before Christmas, and if something didn't happen soon, suppose even *Santa Claus* himself couldn't find her! Santa Claus had lots of things to do. Suppose he didn't have time to look twice, and went right by?

If only Grandmother MacMillan could help! But she was far across the sea, in Scotland. So Wee Ann could only wait and see.

Christmas came closer.

And Wee Ann worried.

And didn't seem to grow any bigger.

And people kept right on saying, "Where is Wee Ann?" when she was right there all the time, as plain as day.

And then, one day it was Christmas Eve.

In Wee Ann's house there was holly, and mistletoe, and there were long pine branches shining with cotton snow.

But Wee Ann hardly noticed.

She asked everybody all over again if they thought Santa Claus could find her if he didn't have time to look twice.

Everyone said they thought he could, but Wee Ann was very worried.

She could hardly eat her supper.

It was almost time for Santa Claus, and all day people had been dropping by to leave presents, and asking "Where is Wee Ann?" when Wee Ann was right there all the time.

And then, right after supper, all of a sudden there came a very loud ring from the front doorbell.

Wee Ann ran to open the door. There on the doorstep stood a Parcel Post Man with a big Christmas smile.

"Miss Emily Ann MacMillan Smith?" he asked. And he handed her a big flat box.

It was a present from Grandmother MacMillan, and it had come all the way across the sea from Scotland!

Right on the top was a letter, addressed to Wee Ann, and it said "Open This On Christmas Eve! Handle With Care."

Wee Ann was so excited she could hardly wait for Mother to read it. Here is what the letter said:

Dear Wee Emily Ann MacMillan:

You can stop worrying about people not seeing you without looking twice, for I have put on my thinking cap. You and I are Scots and we are canny—that means wise. We don't let things worry us when we can do something about them. So I am sending you a present. Open it on Christmas Eve and hang it on your bedpost. Then Santa Claus won't have any trouble finding you, and neither will anybody else when you wear my present. Put it on, eat a big bowl of oatmeal every morning, and I know you'll come to visit me in Scotland very soon.

Love from one MacMillan to another!

Grandmother

When Mother finished reading, Wee Ann could hardly breathe. What could it be?

She cut the string, and took off all the wrappings, and all the bright ribbon.

There in the tissue paper lay the most beautiful, the very brightest plaid skirt in all the world! Only it wasn't really a skirt; it was a kilt, because that is what they are called in Scotland.

"Oh-hh!" said Wee Ann.

She looked and she looked, for the most wonderful thing about it was the color. It was bright red and gay yellow!

It was called MacMillan plaid, because only people whose name was MacMillan could wear it in Scotland. And her name was MacMillan!

It was so bright that now *everybody* could see her, just by looking once!

"O-hh!" said Wee Ann again. And she hugged it tight against her.

It had pleats all around, and a shining silver pin in front, exactly like the kilts they wore in Scotland. And Grandmother MacMillan had sent it just for her!

High on top of her bedpost that night Wee Ann hung her bright Mac-Millan plaid kilt. She wasn't worried any more.

She knew Santa would see it right away.

And he did.

And so does everyone else.

Exactly as Grandmother MacMillan said.

And every morning Wee Ann eats a bowl of oatmeal.

For next summer she is going to Scotland to visit Grandmother Mac-Millan. She is going to wear her MacMillan plaid kilt.

And *everyone* will be able to see her!

139

The Apron Calendar

BY LUCY ELDER*

Grandma Clipperstep made aprons to sell at Christmas time. This year she had seven left over.

New Year's Day came and Grandma did not have a new calendar.

"How can I tell what day it is?" she asked Pixie, her cocker spaniel puppy.

"Why, I know! I'll use my seven aprons.

"I'll wear the blue checked one Monday when I wash.

"The sunny, yellow one can be my ironing apron on Tuesday.

"When I mend and go to Sewing Circle on Wednesday I'll put on the dainty pink ruffled one.

"The green one with the leaves on it will be my gardening apron on Thursday.

"Since Friday is marketing day I'll wear the purple one. The store where I trade has a purple awning out in front.

"I'll tie on the red one Saturday to warn everyone to keep out of my way. I'm too busy then to stop and talk, for I have cleaning and baking to do.

"The white one will be for Sunday, of course. I may have a guest for tea after I get home from church."

So the little old lady folded the aprons and stacked them in order on a chair in her bedroom. Everything went well for a few days. Then one morning she awoke feeling a bit drowsy and saw all of her pretty aprons scattered about the floor. Pixie lay in the midst of them.

"Bad dog!" she scolded. "You've mixed up my calendar!"

The puppy hung her head. Long, silky, blond ears drooped sadly and big brown eyes looked as if they were going to shed tears.

Grandma Clipperstep stooped to pat her head. "Never mind," she soothed. "I'll straighten them out again."

She tied on the purple apron and after the breakfast dishes were done and the bed made she put on her hat.

"Time to buy groceries," she announced to Pixie and started off.

The little old lady looked all about when she got to the store. Her friend, Mrs. Webber, always shopped on Friday too. She didn't come today, though, so Grandma had to go home without a visit this time.

The next morning she put on her red apron and started to clean house and do her baking. She was surprised to see the school children going by with their lunch boxes.

She decided they must be going on a picnic.

Sunday was a day of rest so Grandma didn't get up very early. As soon as she had eaten breakfast she hurried off to church.

Everything looked pretty quiet when she got there. The door was always open so she just went in and sat down. She closed her eyes to rest them for a moment before the other people came.

When the noon train went over the long bridge it awakened Grandma Clipperstep.

"My goodness!" she gasped. "I must have slept through the whole service! I should stop and apologize to the Reverend, but I'd better hurry right home. Pixie will be whining and disturbing the neighbors."

The next morning she arose bright and early. She put on her blue checked apron and started washing clothes. As she hung them on the line she saw people going by all dressed up. They stared a little at Grandma.

141

"I wonder what's so strange about hanging clothes on a line?" she inquired of Pixie.

In the afternoon she remembered that she had to go to the bank. When she got there the doors were locked.

"Must be another of those new holidays," she murmured. "I wonder which one."

The next day she ironed with her little, yellow apron tied about her waist. It made her happy to wear such a pretty thing.

"I certainly wouldn't know what day it was without these aprons to keep me straight," she told Pixie.

The little, pink, ruffled apron was waiting for her the next morning. In the afternoon she wore it to Sewing Circle.

She finished the buttonholes on her new dress and still none of the ladies came. This was the first time she could remember that such a thing had happened.

As she walked out of the hall she saw Mrs. Webber across the street.

"Why didn't you come to Sewing Circle?" the little old lady called to her friend.

"Sewing Circle isn't until tomorrow, Grandma. You must have your days mixed."

"But I don't see how I could," replied Grandma, feeling most embarrassed.

When she got home she counted her aprons. There were only six instead of seven. The green one was missing.

Grandma looked in every drawer and closet in the house. She even peeped into the flour bin and into the medicine chest. Finally she noticed a bit of green peeping out from under the bed.

"Pixie," she cried accusingly, "you hid my green apron the morning you scattered things all over the floor! That's why I'm a day ahead of myself.

"I went to church on Saturday. I washed on Sunday and tried to get into the bank. Today is only Tuesday and I went to Sewing Circle."

The postman whistled. Grandma went to the door and what do you think he had for her? A nice big calendar!

"Thank you," beamed the little old lady. "I sort of made a calendar out of aprons, but it wasn't very dependable."

El Calendario de los Delantales
por Lucy Elder
(Traducido por Leila V. Tossas)

La Abuelita Tijeras hizo delantales para venderlos durante la Navidad. Esta año le sobraron siete. Llegó el Día de Año Nuevo y la Abuelita no tenía un calendario nuevo. "¿Como puedo saber que día es?" preguntó a Píxide, su perrita de aguas. "Pues bien, ¡ ya sé como! Usaré mis siete delantales.
"Usaré el de los cuadritos azules mientras lavo.
"El amarillo, brillante como el sol, puede ser mi delantal el martes mientras plancho.
"Usaré el color de rosa con su delicado rizado el miércoles mientras remiendo en el Círculo de Costura.
"El verde con estampado de hojas será mi delantal el jueves mientras trabajo en el jardín.
"Como el viernes es el día de ir al mercado usaré el de color púrpura. La tienda donde trato tiene un toldo del mismo color en el frente.
"Me ataré el rojo el sábado para advertir a la gente que se aparte de mi camino. No podré pararme a conversar ya que estaré muy ocupada limpiando y horneando.
"Por supuesto que usaré el blanco el domingo. Puede que tenga algún convidado a tomar el te después que regrese de la iglesia."

Por consiguiente la viejecita doblo los delantales y los puso en orden sobre la silla en su dormitorio. Todo iba bien durante unos días. Una mañana se despertó un poco soñolienta y vió todos sus bonitos delantales regados por el piso. Píxide, la perrita de aguas, estaba en medio de ellos.

"¡ Perra mala!" regaño la viejecita. ¡ Confundiste mi calendario! La perrita dejó

143

caer su cabeza. Sus largas y sedosas orejas se doblaron hacia el suelo y parecía que sus grandes ojos derramarían lágrimas.

La Abuelita Tijeras se encorvó y acarició la cabeza de Píxide. "No importa," dijo ella en forma apaciguadora. "Yo los arreglaré y pondré en orden otra vez." Se ató el delantal color púrpura y después de lavar los platos usados en el desayuno y de hacer la cama se puso el sombrero. "Es hora de comprar los abarrotes," anunció a Píxide y salió.

La viejecita miró a su alrededor cuando llegó a la tienda. Su amiga, la señora Webber, también va de compras el viernes. Sinembargo, hoy no vino. La Abuelita regresó a su hogar sin tener con quien conversar esta vez.

A la mañana siguiente se puso el delantal rojo y empezó a limpiar la casa y a hornear. Se sorprendió al ver a los niños yendo para la escuela con sus almuerzos. Ella pensó que a lo mejor iban de pasadía.

El domingo es el día para descansar. Por lo tanto la Abuelita no se levantó muy temprano. Tan pronto terminó de desayunar corrió hacia la iglesia. Como la puerta siempre estaba abierta, entró y se sentó. Cerró sus ojos por un instante antes de que llegara la gente. La Abuelita Tijeras se despertó cuando el tren del mediodía pasó sobre el largo puente. "¡ Ay de mí!" suspiró la Abuelita. "¡ Me he quedado dormida durante todo el servicio!" Debo disculparme con el Reverendo, pero es mejor que me apure y regrese a casa. Píxide se debe estar quejando y molestando a los vecinos.

A la mañana siguiente se levantó temprano y despejada. Se puso el delantal de los cuadritos azules y empezó a lavar la ropa. Según la iba poniendo a secar vió a la gente que iba pasando muy bien vestida. La gente miraba con asombro a la Abuelita. "¿ Qué de extraño tiene el que ponga la ropa a secar?" interrogó la Abuelita dirigiendose a Píxide.

Durante la tarde recordó que tenía que ir al banco. Cuando llegó al banco las puertas estaban cerradas. "Debe ser otro de estos nuevos días feriados," murmuró ella. "Me pregunto cual será."

Al día siguiente se ató el delantal amarillo alrededor de la cintura y se puso a planchar. Usar un artículo tan bonito la hacía muy feliz. "A la verdad que sin estos delantales no me sería posible saber que día es," dijo a Píxide.

El pequeño rizado delantal color de rosa estaba esperando por ella a la mañana siguiente. Se lo puso por la tarde y se fué al Círculo de Costura. Terminó los ojales de su nuevo vestido y las señoras del Círculo de Costura no llegaban. Era la primera vez que una cosa como esta sucedía. Al salir del zaguán vió a la señora Webber cruzando la calle.

"¿ Por qué no vino usted al Círculo de Costura?" preguntó la viejecita a su amiga. "El Círculo de Costura no se reúne hasta mañana, Abuelita. Usted debe haber confundido los días." "Pero no comprendo como ha podido ser eso," replicó la Abuelita, al mismo tiempo que se sentía muy avergonzada.

Cuando llegó a su casa contó los delantales. En vez de siete sólo pudo contar hasta seis. Faltaba el delantal verde. La Abuelita buscó en cada gaveta y armario de la casa. Hasta miró en el arcón de la harina y en el botiquín. Finalmente notó un pedacito de tela verde que sobresalía debajo de la cama. "Píxide," gritó acusadoramente, "¡ escondiste mi delantal verde la mañana que regaste las cosas por todo el piso! Por eso es que me he adelantado un día."

"Fuí a la iglesia el sábado. Lavé la ropa el domingo y traté de entrar al banco. Hoy es solamente martes y fuí al Círculo de Costura."

Sonó el pito del cartero. La Abuelita fué a la puerta y ¿ qué creen ustedes que el cartero le traía? ¡ Un calendario grande y primoroso! "Muchas gracias," dijo la viejecita radiante de alegría. "Más o menos hice un calendario con mis delantales pero no resulto digno de mi confianza."

"The Spanish version of this story was suggested and first used by Mrs. H. Long of the National City Schools. This translation was done by Dr. L. Tossas of San Diego State College."

146

The Giraffe Who Went to School

BY IRMA WILDE*

In a big old-fashioned house, two ladies had a school where they taught four little girls.

The ladies' names were Miss Bee and Miss Dee.

The four little girls were Mary, Ann, Nancy and Pam.

They learned how to read and write and sew.

They learned to sing and dance.

They had French lessons too, and were taught to say, "Pardonez-moi," which means "Pardon me," and "Si'l vous plait," which means "If you please."

Everyone thought the children had lovely manners.

Now, down the road from Miss Bee and Miss Dee's school was a small zoo, where Alice the tame giraffe lived. Every day she would stretch her long neck out as far as it would go—which was pretty far—and look over to where Mary, Ann, Nancy and Pam were playing games and reading books under the big trees in the yard.

"Oh, if I could only go to school, too," sighed Alice. "I would be so good and study so hard. Oh, I wish I could go to school!"

So one day she got up very early, walked out the front gate, down the road, and followed Mary, Ann, Nancy and Pam right up to the schoolhouse.

Miss Bee and Miss Dee were rather surprised, for they had never had a giraffe to teach before.

*Reprinted from "Read-Aloud Kindergarten Stories" by Irma Wilde with the permission of Wonder Books, Inc., © 1957.

"Please, please, Miss Bee," said Mary and Ann. "Please let Alice stay."

"Please, please, Miss Dee," said Nancy and Pam. "Please let Alice stay."

So Miss Bee and Miss Dee said they would be delighted to have Alice in their school.

"Now we will all stand up straight and tall and sing 'America,'" said Miss Bee.

Alice held her head up high like the children, but—OUCH—it bumped the ceiling!

"Now we will sit in a circle and read," said Miss Dee.

Alice tried and tried, but she simply couldn't get comfortable in her little chair. And as for reading—well, big as she was, Alice just couldn't learn her A B C's.

"Perhaps Alice can learn to count," said Miss Bee and Miss Dee hopefully.

But, no, poor Alice couldn't remember what came after ONE. As for real arithmetic, like 2 plus 2 and 3 times 3—why, it made her dizzy just to think about it.

"Never mind, Alice," Mary, Ann, Nancy and Pam comforted her. "We are going outside to play games now, and we're sure you'll do that beautifully."

But Alice tramped on Miss Bee's toe when she tried to play I-Put-My-Left-Foot-Out

And when they played London Bridge, Alice got her long neck all tangled up and upset the little girls.

"We are so sorry," said Miss Bee and Miss Dee, "but Alice will have to go back to her own home at the zoo."

"Then she won't be here tomorrow for May Day and dance around the Maypole with us," cried Mary, Ann, Nancy and Pam. "Oh, dear, oh, dear!" Everyone was sad. Alice was the saddest of all as she went home to the zoo.

Big tears fell down her cheeks the next day when she stretched her neck out and saw the children gathered around the Maypole. They looked lovely and she wanted so much to be with them instead of just looking on.

Suddenly a little breeze started to blow, and it blew and blew and blew itself into a great big wind.

It blew the four little girls' hair ribbons and sashes. And it blew Miss Bee's frilly blouse. And it blew Miss Dee's ruffles on her skirt.

Worst of all, it blew the Maypole right out of the ground, up into the air, and out of sight over the treetops.

Miss Bee grabbed Mary and Ann, and Miss Dee snatched Nancy and Pam just in time to keep them from blowing away too.

So the wind went away with the Maypole. What a dreadful thing to happen! Whoever heard of a May Day without a Maypole? And what in the world were they to do? Miss Bee was distressed, and Miss Dee was distracted, and Mary, Ann, Nancy and Pam were so disappointed that they cried.

But Alice had been watching everything right from the zoo, "I wonder," thought Alice. "Could I help? I wonder—maybe I could! I wonder—yes, I'll do it!"

She raced down the road. She ran into the garden.

"Quick," said Alice to Miss Dee, "get more flowers."

"Quick, quick," said Alice to Miss Bee, "get more ribbons."

"Quick, quick, quick," said Alice to the children. "Fasten them on my head. I will be your Maypole!"

So Mary, Ann, Nancy and Pam danced around Alice and sang their May Day songs.

They sang and sang, and danced and danced, and it was the best May Day that Mary, Ann, Nancy and Pam ever had.

"And Alice is the best Maypole we have ever had," Miss Bee and Miss Dee agreed.

"Even if Alice can't read and count and play games, she can be the most beautiful Maypole in the world," said Mary, Ann, Nancy and Pam.

This made Alice very, very happy. She thought it was the very best thing anyone had ever said about her, and after this wonderful day she knew she would always be happy in her home at the zoo.

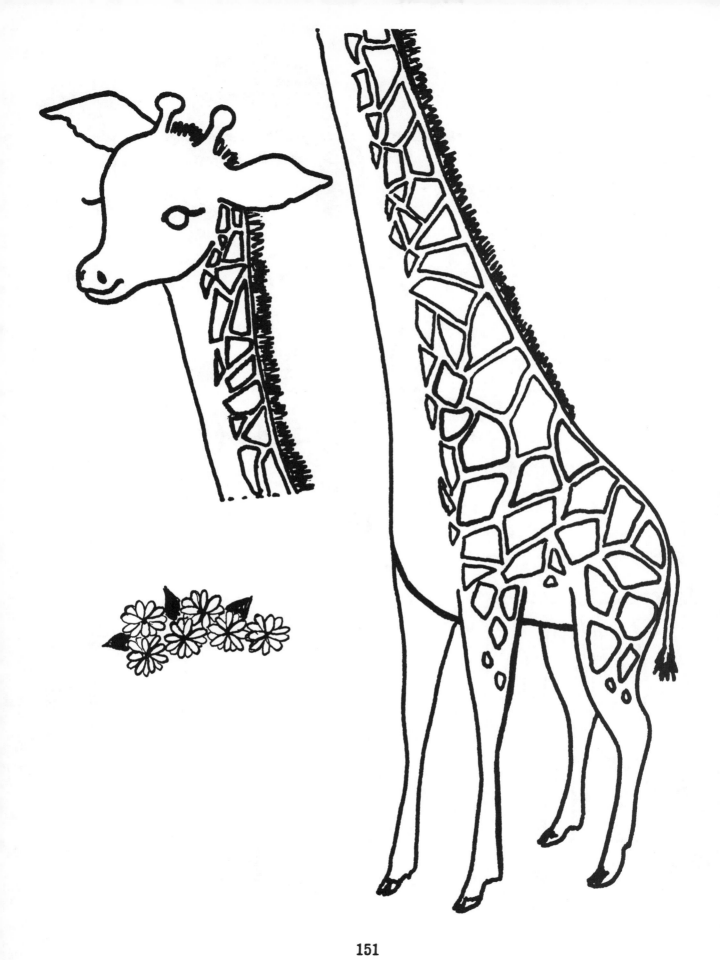

151

Make four girls.

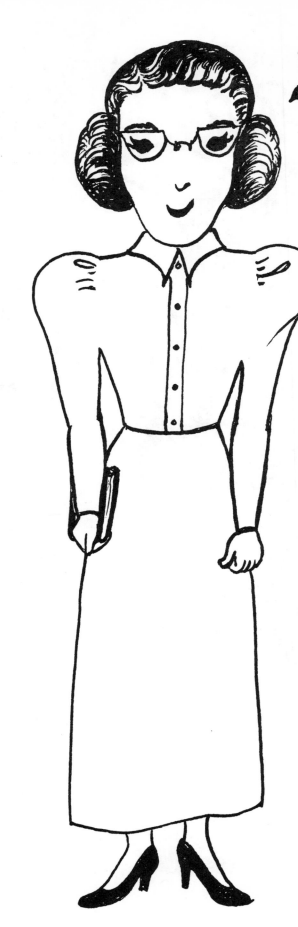

Make pole twice this height.

Attach narrow crepe paper streamers to top.

Make four girls.

Florry Skywriter

BY MABEL WATTS*

Florry was born in an airplane factory, and when she was finished everyone gathered around and decided she was most satisfactory.

"She's neat and trim," said a factory worker.

"She's full of vim," said another.

"She will fly," said a third. "Like a bird!"

These compliments all went to Florry's head, so that by the time she took off on her trial spin she had quite an opinion of herself

She thought she was the finest, the fastest, and the cleverest plane that had ever been turned out.

So Florry tried her wings for the very first time. And goodness me, you would have thought she owned the sky!

She did loop the loops and barrel rolls till Joe the pilot almost went crazy. "Do you want to crack up before I've even tested you?" he yelled.

After that Florry behaved a bit better. She showed Joe she could fly very well, when she had a mind to.

"You're okay," said Joe, when the trial spin was over. And he christened her Florry Flyright, because he thought she was going to be that kind of a plane.

Florry liked being an airplane. Then one day she found out something most unpleasant. She discovered that airplanes all worked!

*Reprinted from "Read-Aloud Kindergarten Stories" with the permission of the author and Wonder Books, Inc., © 1957.

Some carried passengers. Some carried mail. But all of them worked from motor to tail. And some, she learned, the most venturesome and spry . . . were taught how to write in the sky!

One day Florry found out that she was going to be a skywriter, too.

"The first thing you have to learn about being a skywriter," said Joe, "is to learn how to spell!"

So the next morning Florry went to school upstairs in the sky. There were many other planes in Florry's class. And they were all learning to be skywriters, too.

"You youngsters have a lot to learn," said the teacher plane. "But these are the most important things:

"You must memorize your ABC's. . . . You must mind your P's and Q's. . . . And always dot your I's and cross your T's."

"Lessons are a nuisance," Florry told Joe. And she traced a game of tic-tac-toe.

"Get back to class this very minute," yelled Joe, "or the teacher will put you in a corner of the sky!"

Joe tried to make a good little skywriter out of Florry. But Florry played around all the time. She wouldn't work at her spelling lessons at all. And she began to get very poor report cards.

She got F in spelling, and F in writing, and F in deportment. F meant failure, you know. It meant that Florry hadn't been trying.

In the meantime the other little skywriters were going right ahead.

They knew how to write: "PETE'S FOR EATS" . . . "HUGHES FOR SHOES" . . . and "WISE FOR PIES."

They could trace "PETER'S PILLS CURE YOUR ILLS!" clear across the sky.

But Florry couldn't even write her name. All she could do was to doodle in the blue!

"You are a very poor student," the teacher told Florry. "In plain words, you are a dunce. And the penalty for being a dunce is this—no play on Saturday!"

No play on Saturday, thought Florry. Why, this was awful! The pilots always took the little skywriters out on Saturday afternoons. They took them way up to the bluest part of the sky, to the plane playground.

There the little skywriters did barrel rolls and loops to their heart's content. And on the way back to the airfield they jumped treetops and fences and weather vanes.

Florry loved to go to the plane playground. But sure enough, the very next Saturday she was grounded. "No work, no play. . . . That's what I say," said Joe.

And away he went, leaving Florry in her hangar.

This unfortunate turn of events made Florry mad. She stamped her wheels and gnashed her propeller, and rattled her fuselage.

"If Joe won't take me out to play," she declared, "then I'll go by myself!"

Florry started up her motor . . . Putta-putta-put . . . WHIRRR! And soon she was way up in the bluest part of the sky with all the other little skywriters.

Florry did tumbles and twists and sharp turns all over the place. She played "steeple tag" and "snap-dragon" with the other little skywriters.

Then the other planes went home, and Florry had the whole big sky to herself. "Now I'll really have a time," she told herself. And she flipped and turned and raced around the sky till she was almost out of gas.

"What will I doooo?" cried Florry. "Whatever will I doooo now?" Florry popped into a cloud to think a bit. "I'll write for help," she decided at last. "After all, I AM a skywriter!"

Florry started to trace a trail of smoke. "Let me see now," she frowned. "How do you spell, 'Help' ?"

But Florry had never gotten out of the kindergarten. She didn't know an "H" from a hole in the ground, so she couldn't even start to write "Help!"

"Might as well be 'Helicopter,'" cried Florry, "because I can't spell that either!"

PTTT . . . SPTTT . . . PTTT . . . FTTT . . . Not a drop of gas!

"Serves me right," spluttered Florry. "This is what I get for not learning how to spell."

With that Florry went into a terrible, terrible tailspin.

Down, down she spiraled . . . ZZZZZ . . . ZZZZZ . . . CRASH!

And the next thing Florry knew she was back in the airplane factory getting her wings patched up.

"That's what happens to little skywriters," Joe told her, "when they won't learn their ABC's . . . when they won't mind their P's and Q's . . . and when they won't dot their I's and cross their T's."

"I've learned my lesson," throbbed Florry. "Give me just one more chance, and I'll show you what a good little skywriter I can be!"

"Just one more chance," said Joe. "And that's all."

And the next morning Florry went back to school, upstairs in the sky.

After that the little skywriter worked very hard. She learned to write: "JEAN'S FOR BEANS" . . . "SPRATT'S FOR HATS" . . . and "CHET'S FOR PETS."

She learned to trace: "GINGER POP MAKES YOU HOP," clear across the sky!

And guess who won the spelling bee in Florry's class last week? Why, it was Florry, of course.

She was the only little skywriter who could spell "MISSISSIPPI" backwards . . . and dot all the I's!

This was a pretty clever thing to do!

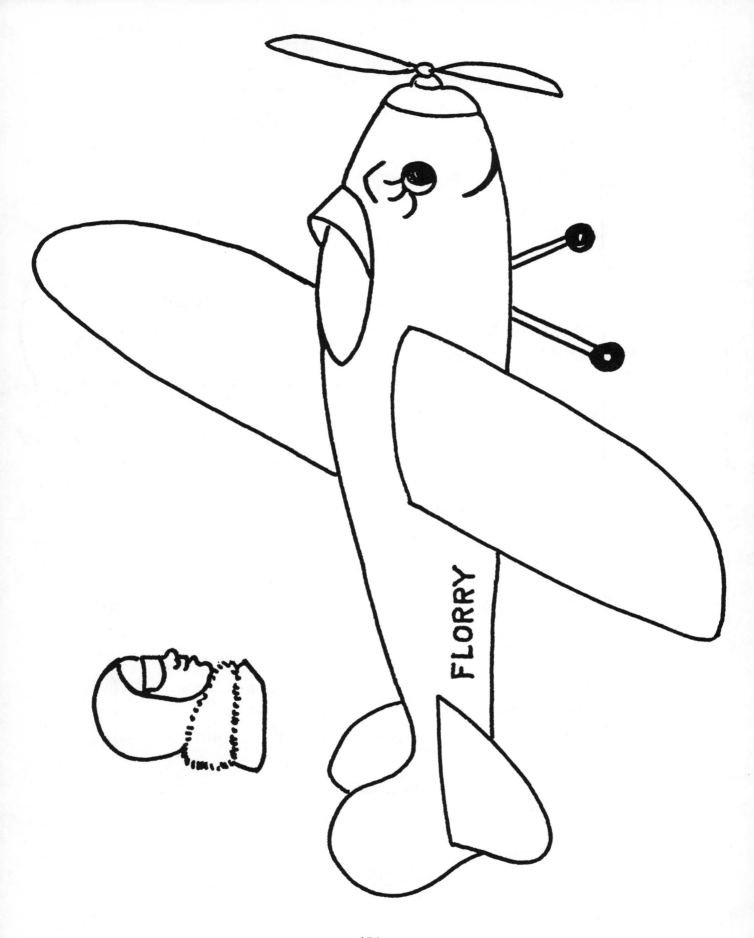

FLORRY

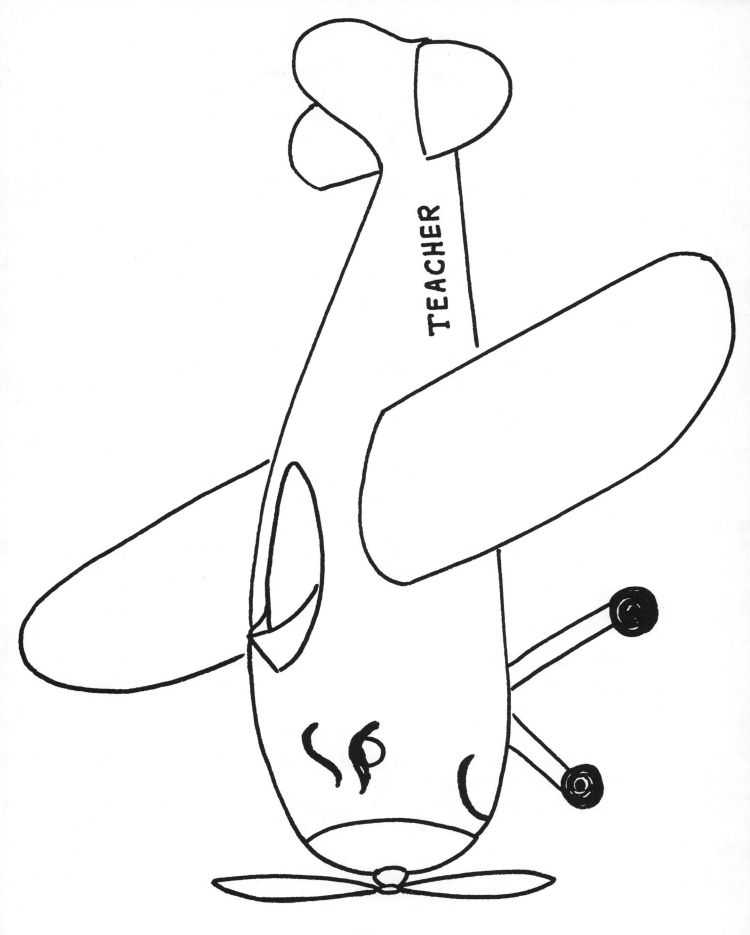

The Winter Picnic

Detroit Kindergarten Teachers

A NOTE TO THE TEACHER:

As you read this story with your children, let them count the number of rabbits, squirrels and chipmunks and other objects in each word picture.

One winter day *5 rabbits* went hop-hop-hopping through the snow. They were going to visit the *4 squirrels* who lived in the *2 trees* down by the *lake*. Each *rabbit* carried a basket, and each basket had *5 nuts* and *2 carrots* in it.

On the way they met *3 chipmunks*. "Hello, *5 rabbits*," said the *3 chipmunks*. "Where are you going?"

"Over to the *2 trees* by the *lake*. We're going to have a winter picnic with the *4 squirrels*," they said. "Why don't you come, too?"

The *3 chipmunks* hopped into their *house*. Then out they came with *3 bags*. In each *bag* they had *2 apples* and *5 nuts*.

"Now we'll have plenty to eat," said the *5 rabbits*. What a funny parade they made with *5 rabbits* hop-hop-hopping through the snow with *5 baskets*, and behind them *3 chipmunks* carrying *3 bags*. At last they reached the *2 trees* by the *lake*.

"How nice!" exclaimed the *4 squirrels* together. "You brought company!" Then *2 rabbits* spread a blanket on the ground, and *3 rabbits* unpacked the *5 baskets*, and *1 chipmunk* unpacked the *3 bags*. After everyone had eaten, the *3 chipmunks* and *4 squirrels* and *5 rabbits* played hide and seek in the snow. All too soon the *sun* began to set behind the *2 trees,* and. it was time to go *home.*

"Come again," called the *4 squirrels* as the *3 chipmunks* and *5 rabbits* went off through the snow. What a lovely picnic!

La Merienda Invernal
(Maestras de Jardin de Inafancia)
Detroit
(Traducido por Leila V. Tossas)

Atención Maestra:
Según usted va leyendo el cuento con sus alumnos, póngalos a contar el número de ardillas, ardillas listadas, y otros objetos presentados en cada lámina.

Un día de invierno cinco (5) conejos se fueron haciendo cabriolas sobre la nieve. Iban a visitar a las cuatro (4) ardillas que vivían en los dos (2) árboles a la orilla del lago. Cada conejo llevaba una cesta, y cada cesta contenía cinco (5) nueces y dos (2) zanahorias.

En el camino encontraron a tres (3) ardillas listadas. "Hola, cinco (5) conejos," dijeron las tres (3) ardillas listadas. "¿ Hacia dónde van ustedas?" "Vamos hacia los dos (2) árboles a la orilla del lago. Vamos a tener una merienda invernal con las cuatro (4) ardillas," dijeron los conejos. "¿ Por qué no vienen ustedes también?"

De un brinco las tres (3) ardillas listadas entraron en su casa. Más tarde salieron con tres (3) sacos. Cada saco contenía dos (2) manzanas y cinco (5) nueces.

"Ahora tendremos suficiente comida," dijeron los cinco (5) conejos. ¡ Qué parada mas graciosa formaron los cinco (5) conejos haciendo cabriolas sobre la nieve con sus cinco (5) cestas y detrás las tres (3) ardillas listadas con sus tres (3) sacos! Por fin llegaron a los dos (2) árboles a la orilla del lago.

"¡ Qué bueno!" exclamaron las cuatro (4) ardillas al mismo tiempo. "¡ Trajeron compañía!" Entonces dos (2) conejos extendieron una manta sobre la tierra, y tres (3) conejos desempaquetaron las cinco (5) cestas, y una (1) ardilla listada desempaquetó los tres (3) sacos.

161

Después que comieron, las tres (3) ardillas listadas, las cuatro (4) ardillas, y los cinco (5) conejos jugaron al esconder en la nieve. Muy pronto el sol empezo a ponerse detrás de los dos (2) árboles, y llegó la hora de regresar a casa. "Vuelvan otra vez," dijeron las cuatro (4) ardillas a medida que tres (3) ardillas listadas y cinco (5) conejos se retiraban avanzando entre la nieve. ¡ Qué merienda mas deleitosa!

"The Spanish version of this story was suggested and first used by Mrs. H. Long of the National City Schools. This translation was done by Dr. L. Tossas of San Diego State College."

Make 5

Make 3

Make 4

163

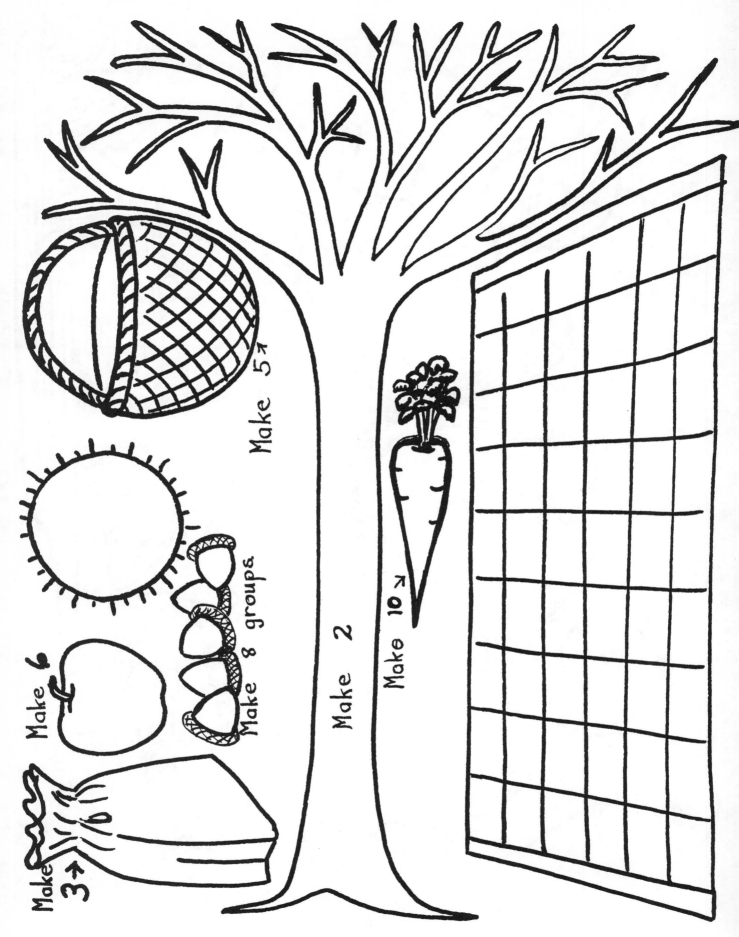

Make 5↗

Make 6

Make 8 groups.

Make 2

Make 10↘

Make 3↗

Teeto, the Tadpole

Detroit Kindergarten Club

Teeto, the tadpole, was born in a large pond with many other little tad-poles. One day his mother went to the edge of the pond and laid her eggs in the cool water. The eggs floated in great green masses near the top of the water.

Each egg was small, round, and light-colored. A black speck showed on each one. The eggs had grown, and now polliwogs were hatching out of them. Teeto was a little fat polliwog. He wiggled and twisted to get out of his egg. He wanted to free himself.

The little fat polliwog got himself free at last and swam around. To his surprise, things began to grow upon him, making him look different. In a few days he had some gills on each side of his head. He could breathe through these. He had a fine tail for swimming, too, and could speed through the water much faster each day. Teeto was very proud of himself and was having such fun with his pals.

Best of all, though, were two little horns or beaks around his mouth. "Ah," he said to himself, "just watch me eat and grow now." Sure enough, the two little beaks were very good for nipping off the green things floating in the pool, and for gobbling up mouthfuls of the mud that had tiny bits of good food in it. "I have to eat and grow," said little Teeto. "I can't be a polli-wog all my life. I'm going to be something much grander."

He grew and grew. After a few weeks he became a full-grown tadpole. He was still very small, but fat and strong. Then it was time for him to

165

change. His gills and tail began to disappear and little legs began to grow. "Good-by, gills and tail," said the little tadpole, "I like my strong legs much better."

Soon he became a small, green frog, with lovely big, wide open eyes and a very large mouth for so little a fellow. He had a smooth, moist skin with lovely spotted colors. Behind his eyes were smooth drumheads that were his ears. He could hear and see very well, indeed. But he could eat best of all. He ate and ate. He liked worms, flies, mosquitos, and other little insects that came his way.

And how he could jump, and swim, and dive! He certainly was glad that he no longer was an egg, or a polliwog, or a mere tadpole. He loved being a grown-up frog and even changed his name from TEETO, THE TADPOLE to FREDDY, THE FROG.

* * * *

Intermediate grade children will enjoy making their own pictures to go with this flannelgraph story.

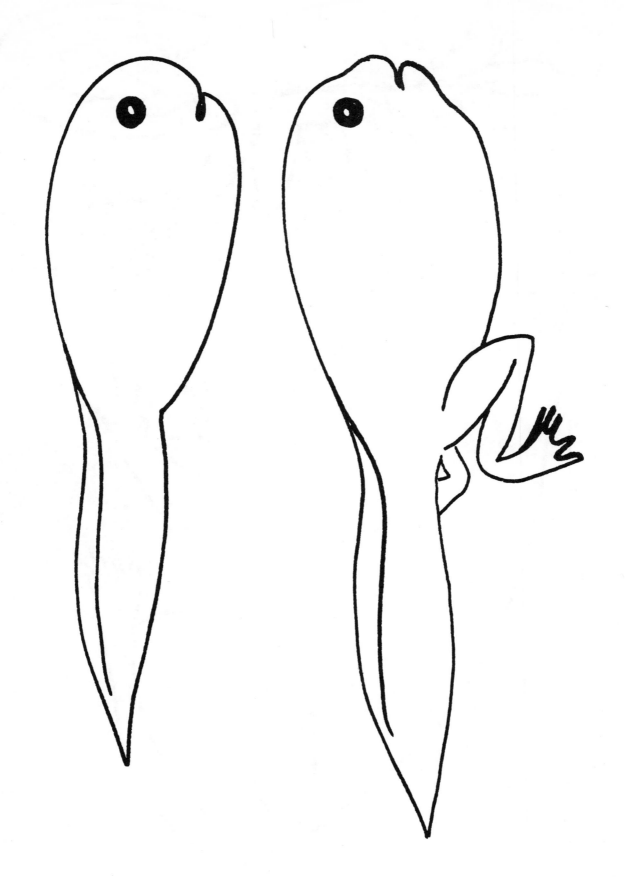

The Boy Who Grew a Halo

BY WILLA BEALL

It happened one morning two weeks before Christmas. Mr. Barlow threw down his paper at the breakfast table and said, "Confound it, where's that glare coming from?"

Benjamin Barlow, busy spooning up cereal, looked up with his mouth full.

Mrs. Barlow tried to look brightly in Mr. Barlow's direction but could not quite manage her eyelids. The sun streamed into the breakfast room over Mr. Barlow's shoulder.

"Glare," Mr. Barlow raised his voice testily.

"You are," said Mrs. Barlow, coming awake all of a sudden. "You're glaring, darling. Though why, I don't know, when it's bright for a winter day, and just two weeks before Christmas."

"Where's it coming from?" said Mr. Barlow, peering around. "I would like to read my paper in peace."

"Move your chair, dear. Benjie, let your father . . ." Mrs. Barlow's voice died away.

"What's the matter?" said Mr. Barlow. He looked over at Benjamin too. He choked. As soon as he recovered, Mr. Barlow said very sternly, "Benjamin, haven't we had enough of propeller hats, quacking duck hats, and radio hats? What's that thing you're wearing?"

Benjamin swallowed before he spoke. "What thing, Father?"

170

"That shiny thing over your head." Mr. Barlow had not had his second cup of coffee and he began to shout. "Take it off, I say. Take it off immediately."

"Just a minute, dear," said Mrs. Barlow. Her eyes were quite open now. In fact, they were popping. Benjamin had been behaving like a model child recently. She didn't think he would purposely try to annoy his father just before Christmas. In fact, he had given up a lot of annoying habits, like slamming doors and sliding down the banisters.

"Just a minute, dear," Mrs. Barlow said again. She got up shakily and went around to Benjamin and stood behind him, staring down at his head.

"It's not a hat," she said.

"Well, whatever it is," said Mr. Barlow, *"remove it."*

"What is it?" said Benjamin. "What *are* you talking about?" And he reached up his hands to feel.

"There is something, isn't there?" Mrs. Barlow said.

Benjamin was grinning. "It feels like springs," he said. "I try to pull it down and it jumps away. Where's a mirror?"

Over Benjamin's head Mr. and Mrs. Barlow stared at each other. "What in thunderation . . ." said Mr. Barlow. "Good heavens!"

He groped his way around the table, looked down on Benjamin, removed his glasses, looked, took off his glasses, polished them with a handkerchief, put them on and looked again.

"Let me see. Let me see," cried Benjamin. He ran into the hall and looked at himself in the mirror.

"It shines," said Benjamin.

"It's ridiculous," said his father.

"Nevertheless," said his mother, "it's there."

Mr. Barlow was beginning to be worried. "How do you feel, son?" he asked anxiously. "I mean, you're not feverish, are you? Your head doesn't hurt? Stick out your tongue. Maybe we should call the doctor."

Benjamin said, "A-ah," but his throat looked fine.

"We don't want you getting anything just before Christmas, angel," his mother put in.

"Angel," snorted Mr. Barlow. "That explains the whole thing. Why, I ask you, does a boy turn angelic at Christmas? Because he wants an electric train, that's why. He wants an electric train!"

Mrs. Barlow stared at Mr. Barlow in admiration. "A special 'Now-he's-ready-for-an-electric-train' Christmas. You're right. Benjie doesn't even have a Christmas list. All he wants is an electric train."

Just then the telephone rang. "It's Jimmy's mother," said Mr. Barlow a minute later. "Jimmy wants Benjie to come over. You're not going to let him go out—with that—that thing—are you?"

"I want to show Jimmy," cried Benjamin. "Will he be surprised!"

"I'm not sure . . ." began his mother. Then she thought of Mrs. Turner whose children always had more A's and everything than anybody else's children. Now Benjamin had something they didn't have.

"Let's be sensible about this," she said. "Besides, Benjamin has to have fresh air, doesn't he?"

She went to the telephone. "Hello, Mrs. Turner," she said. "Yes, Benjie may come over. He has something to show Jimmy. You'll never guess what. A halo!"

Once Benjie was outside, children came running from up and down the street to stare, to exclaim, to admire.

"Where did you get it, Benjie?"

"May I touch it, Benjie?"

"Oh, I want one, too. I want one, too."

Then they all made a procession with Benjie at the head and spiraled along the sidewalk. "Benjie's got a halo. Benjie's got a halo."

Soon the Barlows' telephone began to ring. All the telephones in town began to ring. All the children in town wanted halos just like Benjie's and, when Mrs. Barlow said apologetically she didn't know where the halo came from, the other mothers said, "Well, if that's the way she was going to act . . ." and they hung up in a huff.

Then department stores, hat shops and novelty places started getting calls.

"Halos?" they said. "Halos?" The managers got frantic and started calling the men who supplied them with toys and hats and novelties. "We could sell hundreds of halos," they shouted. "Why haven't you sent us halos?"

But there was not a halo to be had. There was not a halo in town, or anywhere else in the world, for that matter, except Benjamin's. And it made Benjamin a Very Important Boy.

The city newspapers sent reporters to interview him and, when the photographers came to take his picture, Mrs. Barlow hovered over him anxiously and said, "Be sure your halo is on straight, dear."

Benjamin was offered a $100 savings bond by the Wurzbacher Co., makers of "Glo-Glint," to sign an ad which said, "Benjamin Barlow makes his halo bright with Glo-Glint," but Mrs. Barlow said it was not true and so Benjamin did not get the bond.

But Benjamin did get the leading part in his school Christmas play. After all, as the teacher of drama said, he didn't have to *say* a thing, he'd just have to stand there with his halo shining. It would make the performance a complete success.

"I am afraid all this will go to his head," fussed Mrs. Barlow.

"Well," said Mr. Barlow moodily, "hasn't it already?"

Nobody could decide whether Benjamin had the halo because he was so well-behaved or whether he was well-behaved because he had the halo. Certainly he was changed. Mr. and Mrs. Barlow began to worry about it, for these were some of the things he remembered to do. He remembered to get up in the morning without being called. He remembered to hang up his fleece-lined jacket. He remembered to come to the table with clean hands. And he tried his best to keep his hair combed.

After the first couple days Benjamin did not even have to be reminded to wash around his halo.

There was snow for Christmas. The Barlows had a dazzling Christmas tree hung with red paper chains and silvered sycamore balls and tinsel.

Under the tree, running round and round, was Benjamin Barlow's electric train.

There was a cookie jar shaped like a bulldog. "For Mother from Benjamin."

"Just what I've always wanted," said Mrs. Barlow.

There was a music box that played "Jingle Bells." "For Father from Benjamin."

Benjamin had bought them with money he earned himself, charging one penny to touch his halo and two cents to throw a snowball through it.

Once during the day Mrs. Barlow asked Benjamin if he had washed round his halo. "It doesn't seem so bright," she said. But for the most part they were all too busy with Christmas to notice it.

Later they knew the halo had started to grow dim even on Christmas Day. And a week later, holidays over, Mrs. Barlow had to call Benjamin three times before he would even get out of bed. And when he came to the breakfast table, she noticed several things. Two of his three cowlicks were standing straight up in the air, and the halo was gone. There was no doubt about it.

Mrs. Barlow was sorry that they had not been able to keep it for a souvenir. It would have made a nice Christmas tree ornament, she thought.

But Mr. Barlow said, "I don't think we'll ever see it again."

And they never did.

The Whispering Rabbit

BY MARGARET WISE BROWN*

Once in the spring of the year, there was a sleepy little Easter Rabbit who began to yawn, "Oh, hum." And he yawned and yawned and yawned.

BUNNY: "Hmmmmmm . . . I'm so very sleepy." He opened his little rabbit mouth when he yawned till you could see his white front teeth and his little round pink mouth, and he yawned and he yawned . . . until suddenly . . .

BEE: "Bzzzzzzz," a bee flew right into his mouth—he swallowed the bee.

BUNNY: "Oh, me, what will I do? I have a bee in my throat."

OWL: "Hooo-hOOOO," said an old fat owl. "Always keep your paw in front of your mouth when you yawn."

BUNNY: "But what will I do now? There's a bee in my throat."

OWL: "Silly rabbit," said the owl as he flew away.

The little rabbit started to call after him, but as he opened his mouth to speak, the bumblebee curled up to sleep in his throat—and—all he could do was whisper. He met a little yellow duck.

BUNNY: (whispering) "What shall I do? I have a bee in my throat, and he's asleep. I can't talk out loud."

DUCK: "Why, wake up the bumblebee, of course."

BUNNY: (whispering) "How? All I can do is whisper, and I'm so sleepy, and who can go to sleep with a bumblebee in his throat?"

DUCK: "I'll wake him up. Quack—quack—quack."

*Reprinted by permission from *The Golden Sleepy Book* by Margaret Wise Brown. © copyright 1948, by Golden Press, Inc.

BUNNY: "He's still sound asleep."

Then the little rabbit hopped along a little further until he met a little brown bear.

BUNNY: (whispering) "Oh, hum (yawn). Oh, me, please, will you help me? I have a bee in my throat and he's asleep."

BEAR: "Sure, I'll help you. I have a big voice. I'll wake him up for you. Grr-grr-grr."

BUNNY: "Well-l-l-l-l (yawn). Thank you for trying, but he's still asleep."

And off hopped the little rabbit very slowly, for he was so—so—sleepy. Soon he met a little black cat just curling up to go to sleep.

BUNNY: "Pardon me, but, please, will you help me? I have a bee in my throat, and I'm so very sleepy. I just must get some sleep, or I won't be ready to deliver Easter eggs."

KITTEN: "I'll try. I'll talk in my biggest voice. Meow—meow—meow."

BUNNY: "Oh, me, thank you, but I'm afraid that bee is never going to wake up; and all I can do is whisper."

Along came a little lamb and said,

LAMB: "All the better that you can just whisper. You see, I run in the meadow all day and I know a lot about bees. They don't listen to big noises. Here are some nice boys and girls picking spring flowers— maybe they will help you think of a little noise. Ask them."

BUNNY: "Thank you. I will. Boys and girls, can you help me think of any quiet sounds that might wake this bee up?"

Rabbit calls in boys and girls (group or class): after five or ten ideas— then suddenly the little rabbit said:

BUNNY: "Wait a minute. I think I know."

He told them that he thought it was the tiny little click, made hundreds of miles away by a bumblebee in an apple tree in full bloom on a mountain top. It was the very small click of a bee swallowing some honey from an apple blossom. And everyone was very quiet. Not a sound could be heard, and he made that little sound and the bee woke up. He thought he was missing something and away he flew.

And then the sleepy little rabbit and all the sleepy animals and boys and girls

Closed their mouths,
Closed their eyes,
Closed their ears,
And tucked their heads down in a very soft, comfortable way:
And they all went sound asleep.

It was so quiet that they could hear the sound of that little bee getting honey from an apple tree.

Pedro's Christmas Flower

UNKNOWN

"How are you this morning, Mama?" Pedro spoke softly as he bent over the thin white-faced woman who lay on the cot.

"Better maybe—a little better, Pedro," she whispered. "Perhaps I can get up soon—maybe manana, Pedro."

But Pedro knew that it was not so. Each day his tired little mother grew thinner and paler. If only he could have a good doctor come to the little adobe hut. If only there was medicine for her. But medicine cost money and Pedro earned hardly enough for food from the sale of fireweed.

Pedro sighed as he closed the door. Today he must buy beans and if there was enough money left, a small piece of meat. How he would like to buy a Christmas present for his mother! He would buy one of the silver necklaces which the silversmith sold. Or he'd buy a pair of silver earrings. But, alas, that could never be.

Pedro placed the saddle baskets on each side of the little brown burro and led him out of the shed. The sunshine was bright but the air was crisp.

He walked behind the donkey, switching his long stick gently over the animal's back. Now and then Pedro would stop to pick up a piece of dried mesquite or a piece of dead cactus. These he loaded into baskets. But wood was hard to find on the desert. He walked farther than he had ever gone before.

He climbed a little rise of ground and stood on the sandy knoll looking down into the little valley below. A tiny stream trickled from a small rocky cliff. It ran into a little pool. Beside the pool, growing close to the water were some tall pretty red flowers. Their leaves were a glossy green. They shone like the wax candles in the church. Pedro ran down the slope to the flowers.

"They're beautiful," he cried. "Like—like Christmas. I'll pick Mama a bouquet for a Christmas surprise." He bent and picked a beautiful bright red blossom. But almost as soon he he pulled the stalk from its root, it withered. Its petals seemed to shiver and fade. The white sap dripped onto his fingers.

"Oh," Pedro cried, "they bleed. They die! But perhaps if I dig the roots, too, they will keep for Mama's Christmas." He took a sharp stick and dug carefully about the roots. Soon he had a soft ball of earth with the red flower standing proudly upright in the middle. Pedro put the plant in the corner of one of his wood baskets. Then he kept on gathering fireweed. When the baskets were full he turned the little burro back toward home. It was still early when he stopped at the house of his first customer.

"Buenos dias," Senora Martinez greeted him. "What a lovely flower you have there, Pedro!"

"A beautiful flower," said a man who was standing beside the donkey. He was a stranger and had difficulty speaking the language.

"It is for my mama," Pedro said. "It is for her Christmas."

"Dr. Poinsett is a great lover of flowers," Senora Martinez said. "At his home in the United States he has a greenhouse where he raises many flowers."

"But that one," the tall doctor said, "is a new one to me. It is very lovely. Would you sell it, boy?"

"It is for Mama," Pedro said. Then quickly, "But if you are a doctor perhaps you could help me, sir. My mama is very sick and there is no doctor. If you would come, sir, I could show you where these flowers grow. You could have all of them you want."

"You say your mother is ill?" The doctor had forgotten the flower.

"Oh, yes, and white and thin. I try to help her but she needs medicine."

"I will come," the doctor said. "One moment and I will be with you."

The good doctor got his black bag and Pedro led the way to the adobe hut. Pedro waited outside while the doctor made his examination. It seemed a long time before he came out but Pedro was glad to see a smile on his face.

"Good food and the right medicine will cure her. You and I will go into the village and get what she needs. She is very sick now but she will get better soon."

"Oh, Dr. Poinsett," Pedro cried, "you mean she will be well and strong again?"

"Yes," said the doctor, "but she will need fruit and vegetables. Beans are not enough. Come, we will go shopping."

They went to the village and the good doctor bought fruit, vegetables, meat and milk. "You must eat these good foods too, Pedro," said the doctor. "I will bring some each day while I am staying with Senora Martinez. Then I will leave money for you to buy more good food."

"Gracias, gracias," cried Pedro. He prepared the food for dinner and hurried to wash and put away the dishes. Then he put the baskets on the burro and hurried away to the little valley. The sun was going down before he finished digging out the roots of a beautiful red flower like the one he had dug for his mother. He took it to the good doctor.

"Here is your Christmas flower," said Pedro.

"It will be the Christmas flower of many people," said the doctor, "just wait and we shall see."

"It shall be my poinsettia flower," said Pedro. "I shall name it for you. You are making my mother well and we shall have a good Christmas."

"Poinsettia is a good name," said the doctor. "We shall call it that."

So Pedro's red flower is now the Christmas flower, not only to one nation but to many. It is raised all over the country from which it came. Scarcely a cottage in Mexico is without its tall red flowers that almost cover the house at Christmas time. Pedro's flower is truly a great gift.

A Jolly Fellow

BY ARLENE CASTOR GUSTAFSON

Courtesy Speech Course of Study, Los Angeles City Schools

The story may be told with a flannel board and the assembled parts of a Santa Claus figure backed with flannel. Gestures are used to help illustrate the story. Suggested gestures for the following phrases are:

1. "Charles and Susan slept and slept"—resting head on folded hands to opposite side on each of the words "slept."

2. "Whoosh went the wind"—upward movement of hand.

3. "Warm, warm floor"—a downward patting gesture of hands.

4. Hands measure out the size of the "big boots," "short pants," "long jacket," "long sleeves," "fat mittens" (hands up and fingers spread apart), and "long beard." The measurement is increased three times in keeping with the rhythm of the story.

This story starts just like all stories—Once upon a time. Once upon a time there was a boy named Charles, and his sister, Susan. Now it was late one evening in December and time for Charles and Susan to go to bed. Their mother called, "Charles, Susan, it's time for bed." But Charles and Susan asked just what you do sometimes. "Oh Mother, can't we please stay up just a few more minutes?" They wanted to stay up a few more minutes and wait for someone very special to come.

Mother looked puzzled but she said, "Well, just a few more minutes." So Charles and Susan went over by the fireplace where it was nice and warm and each curled up in a big comfortable chair and waited and waited for someone to come. And while they waited they fell asleep. As they slept, whoosh went the wind, and down the chimney into the fireplace dropped two big boots on the warm, warm floor. And still Charles and Susan slept and waited and waited for someone to come.

Whoosh went the wind, and down dropped a pair of short, short pants on the big, big boots on the warm, warm floor. And still Charles and Susan slept and slept and waited and waited for someone to come. Whoosh went the wind, and down dropped a long, long jacket on the short, short pants on the big, big boots on the warm, warm floor. And still Charles and Susan slept and slept and waited and waited for someone to come.

Whoosh went the wind, and down came a pair of long, long sleeves on the long, long jacket, on the short, short pants on the big, big boots on the warm, warm floor. And still Charles and Susan slept and slept and waited and waited for someone to come.

Whoosh went the wind, and down dropped a pair of fat, fat mittens on the long, long sleeves on the long, long jacket on the short, short pants on the big, big boots, on the warm, warm floor. And still Charles and Susan slept and slept and waited and waited for someone to come.

Whoosh went the wind, and then appeard a jolly, jolly face with a long, long beard on the long, long jacket on the short, short pants on the big, big boots on the warm, warm floor. And still Charles and Susan slept and slept and waited and waited for someone to come—but someone was there!

And whom do you think it was? Yes, it was jolly Santa Claus. He hummed a merry tune and busied himself filling up a long, long stocking for mother. Then he filled up a medium-sized stocking for father and then a small stocking for Charles and then a very small stocking for Susan. (With gestures, also measure stockings and packages.)

And with a hearty laugh he turned and went over to the Christmas tree. He put many beautiful shiny packages under it. Some were very tiny packages, some medium-sized packages, and some very large shiny packages.

Then whoosh went the wind, and the jolly, jolly face with the long, long beard on the long, long jacket on the short, short pants on the big, big boots on the warm, warm floor disappeared. And still Charles and Susan slept and slept and waited and waited for someone to come.

Whoosh went the wind, and the fat, fat mittens on the long, long sleeves on the long, long jacket on the short, short pants on the big, big boots on the warm, warm floor disappeared. And still Charles and Susan slept and slept and waited for someone to come.

Whoosh went the wind, and the long, long sleeves on the long, long jacket on the short, short pants on the big, big boots on the warm, warm floor disappeared. And still Charles and Susan slept and slept and waited for someone to come.

Whoosh went the wind, the long, long jacket on the short, short pants on the big, big boots on the warm, warm floor disappeared. And still Charles and Susan slept and slept and waited and waited for someone to come.

Whoosh went the wind, and the short, short pants on the big, big boots on the warm, warm floor disappeared. And still Charles and Susan slept and slept and waited and waited for someone to come.

Whoosh went the wind, and the big, big boots on the warm, warm floor disappeared. And still Charles and Susan slept and slept and waited and waited for someone to come.

Whoosh went the wind, and whoosh went the wind, and whoosh went the wind. And it rattled down the chimney so loud that it woke Charles and Susan. They heard a loud merry voice say, "Merry Christmas to all and to all a good night."

The Child Who Found Easter

UNKNOWN

Once upon a time when the winter was over in the city, there was a child who thought he would like to go out into the street and find out for himself if the spring had truly come. It was a long, crowded street—full of mighty trucks, and day and night these trucks carrying milk and fruit and vegetables rumbled over the road. It was a long and narrow street, crowded with many workers, and from morning till night these people jostled each other as they hurried to their work and home again. It was a long and noisy street, with car horns and grinding, squeaking wheels, and voices—sounds that were never stilled. But this was the child's street and he loved it. It had given him a bunch of lilacs in the summer, a bag of roasted chestnuts in the fall, and an orange and toy in winter. So he decided to go down the long stairs from his home in a tall building to walk along it.

His mother was cleaning the glass in their window when the child started. All winter the coal dust and the soot from the factory chimneys had darkened the window, but now it was bright and clear and the golden sunshine was reflected on the floor. His mother smiled as she worked and she kissed the child saying, "Don't be gone long and be careful on the busy street."

"I'll come back soon after I have asked the street cleaner at the corner if this nice weather will last." And the child gave his mother a hug and skipped down the flight of dim stairs and ran out into the long. narrow and noisy street.

"Hoo hoo, Street Cleaner," shouted the child to his friend with the broom and little white cart. "What kind of weather will we be having?"

Street Cleaner stood at the crossing of the street that he had swept clean, and motioned to the child to come close. He put one hand under the child's chin and tilted his head up, and pointed toward a roof. The child saw a beautiful fluttering butterfly trying its new wings in the city sunshine. The yellow butterfly had burst its winter chrysalis and was trying out its frail wings. "A sign," said the street cleaner. " 'Tis spring."

"A butterfly in our street! Perhaps tomorrow will be Butterfly Day," laughed the child, and this was such a happy thought that he decided to go on down the street to ask his friend, the apples-and-oranges lady, about the weather. He ran along singing, even though his voice was small against all the city noises. He jumped and hopped, and took a kind of rabbit road in and out of the crowds and the trucks and the cars. And presently the child reached the place at the corner where the traffic policeman worked. All the trucks had stopped. All the cars and buses were stopped. The traffic policeman had his gloved hand raised and the child looked to see why all the traffic had been stopped. There in front of the first trucks and cars was a yellow pool of grain that had fallen from a feed wagon. Around it, chirping and cooing, were many kinds of birds. The policeman led the child toward the birds.

"A sign," he said. "Spring has come. See all the birds." And as the birds flew away they sang as if they were trying to say, "Thank you."

"Perhaps tomorrow will be Bird Day," laughed the child, and he went on toward the apples-and-oranges lady. But she had changed. Sure enough, she was wearing the same patched coat and the same faded hat but she had flowers instead of fruit—red tulips and yellow daffodils, pink hyacinth and white daisies.

"Here you are," said the child. "And what will the weather be?" he asked.

The lady smiled and acted as if she knew a secret. She reached into her cart and pulled out a little flower pot with a bright red geranium.

193

"Here," she said. "Give this to your mother, and ye know what kind of day 'twill be."

"Oh, thank you. It will be Flower Day," laughed the child, and he started toward home. Home through the long, crowded, narrow, noisy street the child hastened, remembering what wonders he had seen. A yellow butterfly, birds singing, beautiful flowers, kindness in people's hearts. It was more than spring. All of the city had given him a new feeling in his heart.

His mother had finished cleaning the window and it shone with brightness. It was almost as bright as his mother's smile as he handed her the plant.

"Tomorrow will be Easter Day," he cried. And he knew, from all he had seen and felt, what Easter really means.

The Lavendar Bunny

IRENE FRANCIS

Mrs. Rabbit's eyes became round and wide with surprise. Her mouth dropped open and she became very excited. Then she exclaimed, "What is this? It has two long ears. It has a white fluffy tail. It has funny purple eyes, and . . . IT IS LAVENDAR! My other babies are all white, but this one! ! ! ! What is it?"

It wiggled its little pink nose and looked at Mother Rabbit. Its purple eyes seemed to get larger as they filled with tears. One tear trickled down its pink nose and fell—ker-splash—right at Mother Rabbit's feet. When Mother Rabbit saw the tears she tried to comfort her lavendar baby by saying, "My baby! My beautiful lavendar baby! I've always wanted a lavendar baby!" Then she gave him a big bunny hug. Lavendar Bunny wiggled his nose and blinked his purple eyes, to shake away the tears. He smiled a funny twisted smile, wrinkled his nose, and giggled. Four other giggles joined his giggle. Then, quick as a wink, the five little bunnies were laughing and playing happily together.

Days and weeks went by. Lavendar Bunny loved to play with his brothers and sisters, but he was always a little sad, because he was different. He looked at his two brothers and his two sisters. They were as white as snow with pink eyes, pink noses, and pink ears. He wished with all his heart that he could be like them. He didn't like being different. . . . He didn't like it at all! Then he thought, "Somewhere, someplace, there must be another bunny just like me!"

One day, when the sky was blue and sunny,

He said to himself, "This is the day I'll find that lavendar bunny!"

So he hummed to himself, as he hopped along,

And these are the words of his happy song,

"I'll hop along until I see

Another bunny who looks like me."

He hopped along so merrily,

Till he stopped in the shade of a tall oak tree,

In whose branches was sleeping an owl,

That is, till our hero began to howl,

"I'll hop along until I see

Another bunny who looks like me."

His song was so loud that by and by,

The old owl sleepily opened one eye! ! ! !

He blinked ten times, in great surprise! ! !

Then opened wide, his big round eyes! ! !

"Bunnies just aren't lavendar!" he said,

As he turned loose of the branch and fell on his head.

Reddy Woodpecker looked down from his telephone pole,

Where he had been pecking a deep, deep hole.

He gloomily said, "I've quite a notion

Of the cause of all this commotion.

I've been working in a place that's much too sunny,

For surely, I'm not seeing a lavendar bunny!"

Lavendar Bunny was much too unhappy to cry.

So he softly said, "Oh, me! Oh, my!

Would you please be so kind,

As to tell me of this bunny I'm trying to find?

Did either of you ever see

Another bunny who looks like me?"

The owl smiled kindly and looked very wise,

"This I have seen with my very own eyes—

A bunny that's pink, or sometimes blue,

Or sometimes green, or lavendar, too.

It may seem queer and very, very funny,

But I have seen—THE EASTER BUNNY! ! !

He comes to see children, just once every year,

To bring pretty eggs and loads of good cheer!"

Reddy nodded his head and rapped on a tree,

"Everyone likes him, especially me!"

"You mean no one laughs because he's different and funny?"

This was wonderful news to the Lavendar Bunny.

The old owl exclaimed, "Why should we mind?

He works very hard and is exceedingly kind."

"He likes pink, and yellow," Reddy said.

"But I think he would look best if he were red."

"Wait," said the owl, "I have a plan,

You should paint eggs as fast as you can.

Then no one would think that it is funny

For you to be a lavendar bunny."

"Great!" he said, "I'll find a brush

And paint lavendar eggs—I really must rush!

Tomorrow is Easter, as you well know,

So, just watch me go—go—go!"

He made a mountain of lavendar eggs,

And then to hide them—he needed ten legs!

The owl and the woodpecker were beginning to worry,

They had never seen a rabbit in such a hurry.

Said the owl to the woodpecker, "Between me and you,

I think that rabbit is in a stew!"

When he hid the last egg, it was the middle of the night.

Lavendar Bunny was so happy—He had done something right!

Everyone will be so pleased, just you wait and see!

That no one will think of laughing at me!

Early Easter morning, when the sun was warm and bright,

He heard the children's laughter and their squeals of great delight.

So many pretty eggs were in the bushes, grass, and flowers,

That Easter Bunny must have been busy for hours upon hours!

Place a big basket by the flannel board. Give each child an egg, but have only one lavendar egg. It should be the prettiest. "Some children found red eggs." Those with red eggs will place them in the basket, etc. The lavendar egg is the last egg to be brought forward.

"Such a beautiful egg! What a lovely surprise!"

The children could hardly believe their eyes.

"This is the prize egg!" the children all said.

Lavendar Bunny turned around twice and stood on his head!

This was indeed his happiest day,

For he had made others so merry and gay.

On an Easter egg hunt, the one who spies

Such a beautiful egg, will get a prize.

It was a wreath of blue, lavendar and pink,

Which was on the child's head before you could wink.

Lavendar Bunny was so happy, he jumped up and down,

His little back feet were pounding the ground.

The children turned quickly, and immediately spied,

Our Lavendar Bunny, before he could hide.

He was so startled, he just couldn't run,

Then they called to him sweetly to join in their fun.

They put the wreath upon his head.

His heart beat faster, when one of them said,

"You have made such a fuss,

Doing all this work for us,

We want to do something, too.

We want to show that we like you."

They formed a fife and drum quartet,

And somebody blew a clarinet.

Oh, what beautiful music they played!

AND LAVENDAR BUNNY LED THE PARADE!

Make one lavender egg.

Make enough eggs
so that each child
may have one.

4 white bunnies.

1 lavender bunny.

Make a telephone pole and a tree.

Melody, the Musical Bus

An original story by Irene Counts, *a student at San Diego State College*

"Wake up, Melody! It is morning!" shouted Jake as he came into the garage where all the buses slept. Every morning Jake came earlier than the other drivers to clean and polish Melody. As soon as she had been fed her breakfast of gas, oil and water, Jake would drive her around the shed and listen to all her squeaks and rattles.

Melody was a very unusual bus. She wasn't happy unless all of her squeaks were in harmony. If they did not sound well together, her motor would act up, her horn would toot, and she backfired, "Bang! Bang!" until something was done.

Once all the preparations were finished, Melody and Jake set out on their day's journey. First they went past the drugstore, then out past the school, over the hill past Farmer Jones. Then they drove around the hospital and into the center of town. On the way they stopped at thirty-two different places and picked up forty-five boys and girls and brought them to the schoolhouse.

When school was over Melody and Jake would pick up the boys and girls and bring them home again. As they drove along, Melody sang her song of rattles and squeaks. At the end of the day, Jake took Melody into the garage and put her to bed for the night.

One morning Melody woke up before Jake got there. She waited and waited but Jake did not come. The sun rose higher in the sky, and all the other buses began going out to pick up boys and girls. Still Jake did not come. Finally a man that Melody did not know climbed into the bus.

"What does this mean?" Melody wondered. "This man hasn't cleaned me or adjusted my rattles. Where, oh where, is Jake?"

The new driver took Melody over the regular way. With every bump in the road Melody would rattle and squeak. But things did not sound right to the boys and girls. Somewhere Melody was out of tune.

"Oh, dear!" thought Melody. "This will never do. I cannot listen to this terrible sound all day."

So Melody began to cough. Then she began to backfire. Her horn tooted, she coughed some more. The new driver didn't pay any attention to her— he just drove along without caring about Melody. All day long Melody coughed and sputtered.

That night when Melody was back in the garage she thought, "I'll be glad when morning comes and Jake is back again. He knows how to fix my rattles and squeaks so that I will be in tune again."

But the next morning Jake did not come, nor the next, nor the next. In fact, it was beginning to look as if Jake was not coming back at all. The new driver did not clean poor Melody, or adjust any of her squeaks. Each day she sounded worse. She coughed more, sputtered more and her horn wouldn't honk at all.

"I can't drive that bus any longer. It is too old and worn out!" the new driver told the other drivers one day. "All it does is make a terrible noise."

So Melody was put in the garage and left there. Day after day she sat with no oil or water. She couldn't sing; in fact, she could hardly make a sound. She missed all the boys and girls that used to ride with her.

"How will all those children get to school with me in the garage?" she wondered. "Oh where, oh where, is Jake?" Melody cried.

Then she thought, "I must stop this. A grown-up bus should not cry. Besides, I'll get rusty and never be able to run again."

Just then she heard a voice. "What is the matter, Melody?"

It was Jake! He was back!

"How did you get so dirty? I guess you have been left alone too much while I was gone," Jake said, "but I'll fix that." And he got right to work. First he washed and polished the sides of Melody until she looked bright and clean again. Then he put some grease here and there and a little oil on all her rattly places. After that he drove her outside to listen to her run.

"Poor Melody!" Jake said. "You are really out of tune! Where are all my tools?" After he found them, he worked on Melody from front to back. He would oil and twist, then listen. After that he would oil a little more until Melody began to sing again. Then Jake and Melody went for a ride all over the town. Melody was so happy she sang all the way:

Rattle, rattle, rattle and squeak, squeak, squeak.

This is the song that Melody sings.

Rattle, rattle, rattle and squeak, squeak, squeak.

Over the hills and down the lanes.

Rattle, rattle, rattle and squeak, squeak, squeak.

Listen everybody and you will hear her sing.

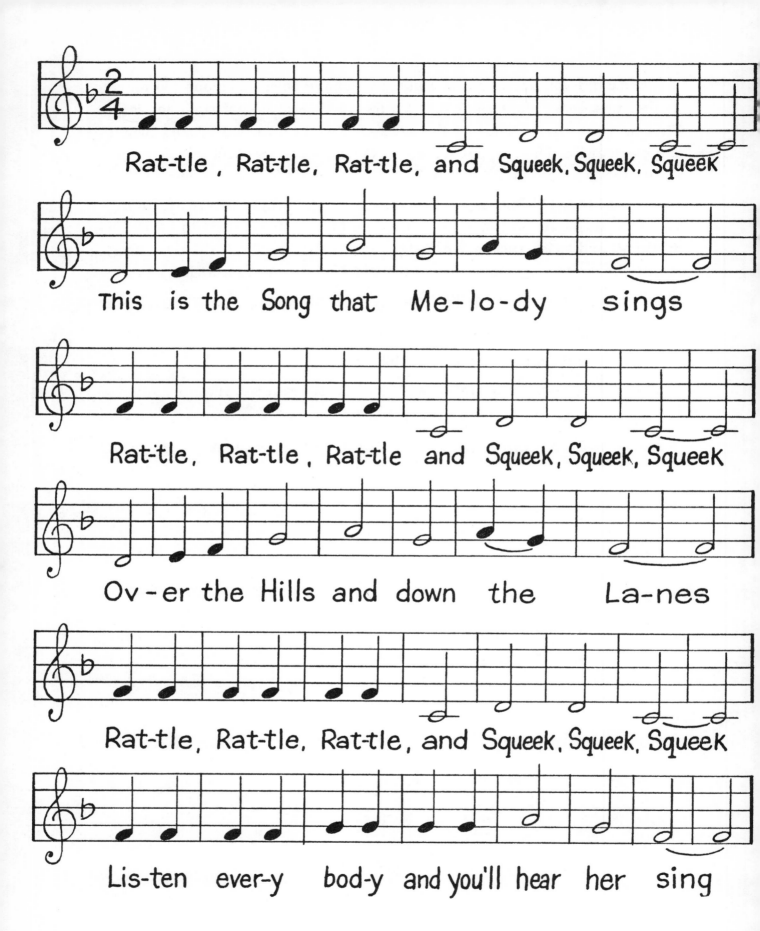

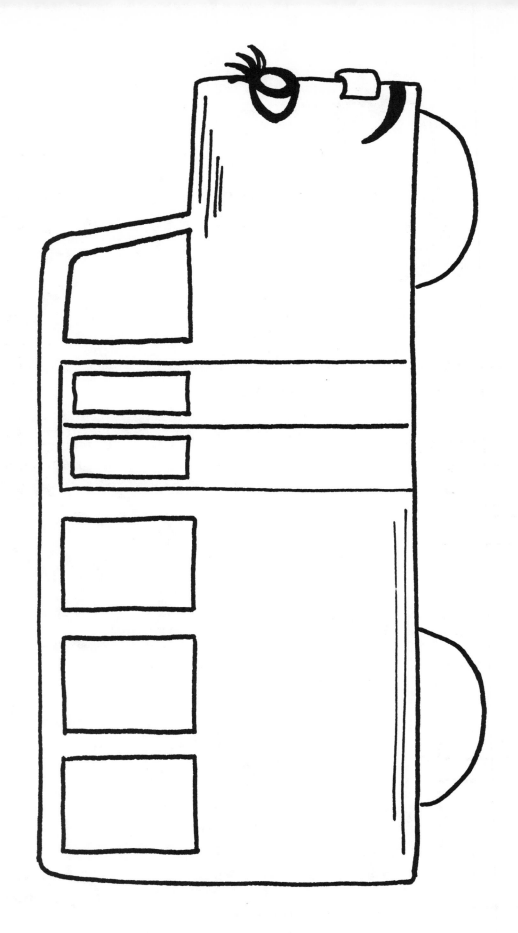

The Thirty-nine Letters

From Story Parade

BY KATHRYN JACKSON

(No characters needed in addition to those provided in other stories. The letters might be written by children.)

When Santa Claus got his first letter from Billy Butters, written by Billy Butters himself, he was tickled pink.

"Look at this," he said to his wife. "Billy Butters has learned to write!"

"Isn't that wonderful!" marveled Mrs. Santa Claus. "It seems no time since you were making a rattle for Billy—and here he is, big enough to write BILLY BUTTERS WANTS A NICE RED SLED, as plain as plain!"

"Yes, sir!" Santa Claus said. "And I'm going to make him the nicest, reddest sled ever!"

Humming to himself, Santa Claus set right to work. He made a fine, strong seat for the sled, and a good, easy-to-steer steering part, and two slick, swift runners.

But just as he was about to fasten the parts together . . . Whizz! Down his chimney came another letter.

"You read it," Santa Claus told his wife. "It will save me time."
So Mrs. Santa Claus read the letter. It said:

BILLY BUTTERS HAS CHANGED HIS MIND. NOW HE WANTS A RED TRICYCLE INSTEAD.

"Well, well," said Santa Claus, pushing back his cap and putting down his screwdriver. "A red tricycle it shall be, then."

Before long, he had made three of the nicest, reddest wheels ever. But just as he was twisting and bending the handlebars . . . Whizz! Down his chimney came another letter.

"I do hope it's not from Billy!" cried Mrs. Santa Claus.

But from Billy it was. It said:

NO! NOW BILLY BUTTERS THINKS A TRAIN WOULD BE THE VERY BEST PRESENT.

"Well, well, well!" said Santa, as he put away the tricycle wheels and reached for some train wheels. "Billy certainly has learned to write, hasn't he?"

"Yes, he has," Mrs. Santa Claus agreed. "But three's the charm, so I expect there will be no more letters from him this year."

But Mrs. Santa Claus was wrong. Charm or no, the letters from Billy kept coming in.

Just as the train was finished, in came a letter asking for a cuckoo clock. Just as the clock was ticking and cuckooing—down came a letter that said:

BILLY BUTTERS WOULD LIKE A NOAH'S ARK BEST OF ALL.

And just as Santa Claus was carving the last Noah's Ark giraffe . . .

Whizz!

   Whizz!

      Whizz!

         Whizz!

Down the chimney came more and more letters from Billy Butters, all changing his mind!

By the time Mrs. Santa Claus had ready Billy's thirty-eighth letter out loud, Santa Claus was muttering to himself.

"I seem to be all thumbs!" he muttered. "Can't even make a plain rubber ball! Oh me, maybe I'm getting too old to be Santa Claus!"

212

"Nonsense!" cried Mrs. Santa Claus. "You just lie down on the polar bear couch, and I'll bring you a cup of hot tea, and you'll soon be feeling fine again!"

But poor Santa Claus tossed and turned, and made faces over his tea. He was sure that he would not be able to make one more Christmas present.

Poor Santa Claus!

He felt so very, very clumsy and mixed-up, that everyone who loved him began to feel mixed-up, too.

Mrs. Butters, who loved Santa Claus dearly, found herself dropping more cookies than she managed to get on the cookie sheet.

"Something's wrong!" she said. "I just seem to be all thumbs!"

"Me, too," said Billy, coming in from school with his boots unzipped. "I couldn't make the zippers work!"

"Well!" his mother said. "Let's have some milk and some freshly baked cookies, and perhaps we'll both feel better."

So Billy and his mother had big glasses of milk, and plenty of warm cookies, and it helped a lot.

"Now I'll go write some more letters to Santa Claus," smiled Billy.

"Some more letters?" cried his mother. "Why, Billy Butters! How many letters have you written?"

" 'Bout thirty-eight, I guess," said Billy. "I like to write."

Mrs. Butters threw up her hands.

"Thirty-eight letters!" she cried. "Why, Billy Butters! You must have poor Santa Claus in a terrible stew! Now you sit right down and decide exactly what you want. Then you write one more letter and say it very plain —and then you stop writing letters to that poor, busy man!"

"All right," said Billy. "And I know just what I want most."

Now Billy wrote his thirty-ninth letter. It said:

BILLY BUTTERS REALLY WANTS THE RED SLED AFTER ALL.

On the envelope he wrote, LAST LETTER FROM BILLY BUTTERS. He put the letter on the window sill.

Whoooo! The winter wind took it and sailed it high over the housetops.

Whizzz! Billy's letter went whizzing down Santa's chimney.

"Dear, dear!" sighed Mrs. Santa Claus. "Another letter from Billy!"

But when she saw the part about the last letter from Billy, she began to smile.

"Look, Santa!" she said. "Here's Billy's last letter!"

"Well, well!" cried Santa Claus, hopping up and reading it. "Well! And he wants the nice, red sled, after all!"

Now it took Santa Claus no time at all to finish that beautiful, strong, swift, red sled.

It took Mrs. Butters no time to finish baking lots and lots of cookies in jolly Christmas shapes.

It took Billy Butters no time to address Christmas cards to all his friends with an ink pen and red ink.

"Well, well," grinned Santa Claus. "Isn't it a fine thing that Billy Butters has learned when to stop writing letters?"

And Mrs. Santa Claus, busily tidying the polar bear couch after all Santa's tossing and turning, said, "Yes, indeed, it just most certainly was!"

Chapter V

Flannel Board Stories for Speech Practice

Our Daily Bread

Adapted by MARCIA C. GOOKIN

A little boy's mother gave him a brown loaf of bread for his breakfast.

The little boy said, "Thank you, Mother. Thank you for my nice brown loaf of bread."

His mother said, "Don't thank me. Thank the miller who made the flour."

The little boy ran to the miller. He said, "Thank you, miller. Thank you for my nice brown bread."

The miller said, "Don't thank me. Thank the farmer. He grew the wheat."

The little boy ran to the farmer. He said, "Thank you, farmer, for my nice brown bread."

The farmer said, "Don't thank me. Thank the rain. I only planted the wheat."

The little boy saw the clouds in the sky. He saw the raindrops falling. He said, "Thank you, rain. Thank you for my nice brown bread."

The rain said, "Don't thank me. Thank the sun. I only watered the wheat."

Just then the sun began to shine. The little boy said, "Thank you, sun. Thank you for my nice brown bread."

The sun said, "Don't thank me. Thank God who made me."

The little boy went back to the table. Then he said, "Thank you, God. Thank you for my nice brown bread."

Five Little Chickens

Said the first little chicken
With a queer little squirm,
"Oh, I wish I could find
A fat little worm!"

Said the second little chicken
With an odd little shrug,
"Oh, I wish I could find
A fat little bug!"

Said the third little chicken
With a sharp little squeal,
"Oh, I wish I could find
Some nice yellow meal!"

Said the fourth little chicken
With a small sigh of grief,
"Oh, I wish I could find
A green little leaf!"

Said the fifth little chicken
With a faint little moan,
"Oh, I wish I could find
A wee gravel-stone!"

"Now, see here," said the mother,
From the green garden patch,
"If you want any breakfast,
You must come and scratch."

—Old Verse

The Two Chicks

Adapted by MARCIA C. GOOKIN

Once there were two baby chicks that wanted to see the world. One was as black as charcoal. One was as white as chalk.

"Cheep, cheep," said the black one. "Let us see the world."

"Chirp, chirp," said the white one. "Let us see the world."

So they set out upon their way.

Soon they met Gray Squirrel. "Chatter, chatter," said Gray Squirrel; "where are you going, chicks?"

"Cheep," said the black one, "to see the world."

"Chirp," said the white one, "to see the world."

Gray squirrel laughed.

The baby chicks went on their way. Soon they met old Dobbin, the horse. He was eating hay. "Champ, champ. Where are you going, chicks?" he asked.

"Cheep," said the black one, "to see the world."

"Chirp," said the white one, "to see the world."

But Dobbin, the horse, went on eating, "champ, champ," and smiled a bit at the silly chicks.

The two chicks were tired. They thought they had traveled so far that they must be nearly to the end of the earth.

"Oh, cheep, we are lost," cried the black one.

"Oh, chirp, we are lost," cried the white one.

But a robin heard them. "Cheerup, cheerup," he cried, and gave them a cherry to eat. "You'll find you way home," he said, "cheerup, cheerup," and he laughed.

"We are so far from home. Why do they laugh?" asked the chicks. Then they went around a bush and what do you think they saw? Their own chicken coop, with mother chicken calling them. They rushed up to her.

"Oh, Mother, cheep, cheep, we have been around the world," said the black chick.

"Oh, Mother, chirp, chirp, we have been around the world," said the white chick. Mother chicken laughed.

"Why, you haven't been out of the farmyard," she said. The chicks looked around. And sure enough, they hadn't!

Make one black
and one white.

Dobbin

Dobbin was a wooden horse. He belonged to Danny and Donna who were twins four years old. He had belonged to them ever since they were tiny babies and they had played with him so much that now he was almost worn out. Poor Dobbin! One leg was broken, one eye was gone, and so were his mane and tail. The wheels had come off his little red wooden stand. Most of all Dobbin needed a coat of paint.

One evening Daddy brought home a new wooden horse. It was larger than Dobbin. It was all shiny with paint and it had a fine black mane and tail. The twins were so pleased that they danced about and clapped their hands.

"What shall we do with Dobbin?" asked Danny.

"I think we might send him to a little boy who has no toys to play with," said Mother. "But of course we can't send him just the way he is. We must paint and mend him."

So Danny and Donna helped Mother mend Dobbin. First they mended the broken leg and put four new wheels on his stand.

Then Mother let them take turns painting Dobbin a beautiful gray, and the stand bright red. Last of all Mother took the paintbrush and gave Dobbin two black eyes, a bridle, a black mane, and some black spots. With the red paint she gave him a red saddle.

"Now he is all ready," said Mother.

"But he has no tail!" said Donna.

Mother took some hairs from an old broom and glued them in the place where Dobbin's tail had been. The hairs were quite short and Dobbin's new tail was so straight and stiff that it made the twins laugh to look at it.

When all the paint was dry, Mother said, "Now we can wrap Dobbin up and send him to his new home." She found a large sheet of paper, stood Dobbin on it, and began to tie up the package. Danny and Donna watched. Soon there wasn't any Dobbin to be seen—not even the straight, stiff, little tail.

"Oh, Mother," cried Donna, "we can't send Dobbin away. He's been with us such a long time."

"Send the new horse instead," said Danny.

Mother looked surprised, but she opened the package and put the new horse in Dobbin's place.

Danny and Donna hugged Dobbin. "We like you ever so much better than the new horse," they told him. Then they took turns riding on his back as they had always done.

"Gee up, Dobbin! Whoa, Dobbin!" they shouted.

Dobbin ran so fast on his little red wheels that it seemed as if he knew he was to stay and play with Danny and Donna a great many more years.

—Adapted from *Told Under the Blue Umbrella*

tail

mane

spots

Make two Dobbins. The renewed Dobbin should be of gray felt so that spots adhere, etc.

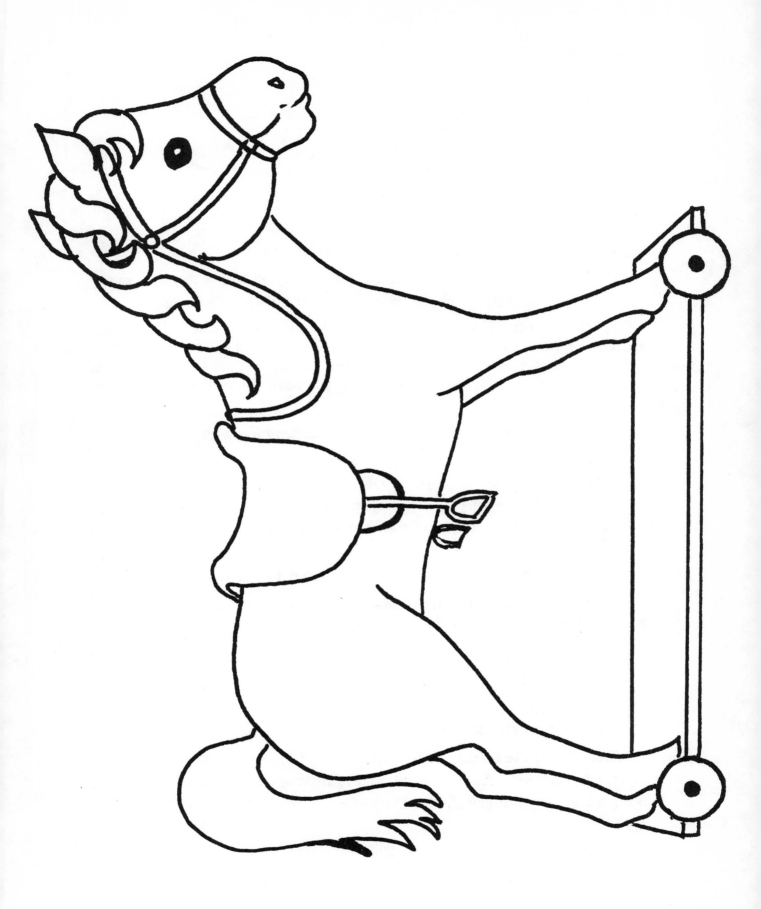

Gerry Goose

(Needed: Goose, goat, crow, girl, farmer, gate.)

This is the story of Gerry, the Goose who wanted to get fat. But every time she went near the cornfield, Gobo, the Goat chased her away.

"Go away, Gerry Goose," he cried, and would not let her eat although there was enough for both of them. Then Gobo would butt Gerry Goose with his horns. Gerry could not get enough to eat to make her fat. What should she do? Gerry Goose walked along the road. Soon she met a black crow.

"Oh, Crow, what shall I do? Gobo Goat chases me away from the corn and I cannot get fat."

"Caw! Caw!" said Black Crow. "Ask the girl coming down the road."

"Oh, Girl, what shall I do?" asked Gerry. "Gobo Goat chases me away from the corn and I cannot find food to make me fat." But the girl did not know what to do.

"Come with me, Gerry," she said. They went to the farmer.

"Farmer," said the girl, "what shall Gerry Goose do? Gobo Goat chases her away from the corn and she cannot find food to make her fat."

"We'll see about that," said the farmer. He took Gerry Goose to the cornfield. Gobo came rushing out of the field to butt Gerry Goose. And what do you think? At that very minute the farmer closed a big gate in the fence so that Gobo Goat could not go back in the field. Gerry Goose was small enough to go through the bars.

"There," said the farmer, "they who will not let others eat shall have no food for themselves." And he went away, leaving Gobo outside the field, looking very, very hungry. As for Gerry Goose, she became very fat indeed.

To make gate:
Fold yellow paper.
Place folded edge
at this side of pattern.→

Carrie Kangaroo

(Needed: Kangaroo, Mrs. Cat, three kittens, cow, cuckoo bird and cuckoo clock, car.)

Carrie was a big mother kangaroo. The farmer bought her from a circus and took her home to his farm. A kangaroo, you know, is a very big, kind animal with small front legs and large back legs on which it runs very fast. And in front, the mother kangaroo has a pocket in her skin where she can carry her baby kangaroo in case of danger. So the kangaroo's name was Carrie because she could carry her baby kangaroo in her pocket.

But all the animals on the farm had never seen a kangaroo before. They thought Carrie was a funny looking animal. They wouldn't be nice to her or to her baby kangaroo. This made her feel very sad.

"I kill mice," said Mrs. Cat in a cross voice. "What can you do?"

"I can carry my baby in my pocket, and run fast, calumph, calumph," said Carrie Kangaroo sadly.

"Oh, pooh," said Mrs. Cat. "That isn't much. I can carry my kitten in my mouth."

"Moo, I give milk. What can you do?" asked the cow.

"I can carry my baby in my pocket and run fast, calumph, calumph," said Carrie Kangaroo sadly.

"Pooh," said the cow. "I can run calumph, calumph if I wish."

Just then a cuckoo bird in a cuckoo clock that heard what the animals were saying, came out of his little door.

"Cuckoo!" he cried.

All the animals laughed. "Yes, Carrie Kangaroo is cuckoo!" they cried. And poor Carrie Kangaroo put Baby Kangaroo in her pocket and went home on her long back legs, "calumph, calumph, calumph."

A few days later, Carrie Kangaroo, leaving her baby at home, was going "calumph" down the road. Of course she was alone because all the animals were so cross to her that she did not like to talk to them. Then she noticed Mrs. Cat's three kittens playing in the middle of the road. Mrs. Cat had told them not to play in the road for a big car might hit them. Carrie Kangaroo saw Mrs. Cat coming to get them, so she went on her way. But all of a sudden Carrie heard Mrs. Cat go "Mew, mew" very loud. She looked back. Mrs. Cat was trying to pick up her kittens in her mouth to carry them out of the road. The three kittens were too frightened to move. And no wonder! Down the road came a great big car! Surely it would run over the three little kittens who were too frightened to move. And Mrs. Cat would have time to carry only one kitten in her mouth to safety.

"Calumph, calumph!" went Carrie Kangaroo. She ran back to the kittens as fast as she could go. And while Mrs. Cat carried one kitten in her mouth, Carrie Kangaroo put the other two in her pocket and carried them off the road before the car could hit them.

Mrs. Cat was so happy that she couldn't stop thanking Carrie. She was sorry for the cross things she had said to Carrie. She told the other animals how brave Carrie Kangaroo had been to save the kittens. The other animals knew they had been wrong. They made Carrie Kangaroo their friend. And the cuckoo clock never called Carrie "cuckoo" anymore.

Make slit.

238

The Three Tops

By Minnie Hill, *Kindergarten Teacher, National City, Calif.*

(A story to be used in teaching the sound "m.")

Once upon a time there were three tops, Father Top, Mother Top, and Baby Top. Father Top was the largest. He was white, brown and orange. His voice was low and heavy when he sang, like this, "M m-m."

Mother Top was smaller than Father Top. She was white, red and blue. She sang like this, "M mm."

Baby Top was the smallest. He was white, green and purple. His voice was light and high. He sang like this, "M m m."

They all lived together very happily in one upstairs room of a large house.

One day Mother Top was making pudding for dinner, and Father Top was reading the newspaper. Baby Top was spinning round and round. "M m m," he sang. What fun he was having!

Round and round he spun, "M m m," right out into the hall. Mother had often warned him about the steps at the end of the hall. "M mm," she had said. "Baby Top, don't spin into the hall. You might fall down the steps."

But Baby Top was having so much fun he had forgotten. Oh, this was such a good place to spin for Mother had just waxed the hall floor. "M m m" on and on he spun until he had reached the stairs. He was spinning so fast he couldn't stop. Bumpity, bumpity bump right down the steps he went.

"M m m," he cried. Mother heard him fall. She spun into the hall and over to the stairs. " M mm," she said. "Are you hurt, Baby Top?" Father spun right after her. "M m-m, are you hurt Baby Top?" he said. "M m m," said Baby Top. "No, I landed on a pillow." "M mm," said Mother Top. "Thank goodness." "M m-m," said Father Top. "Yes, thank goodness."

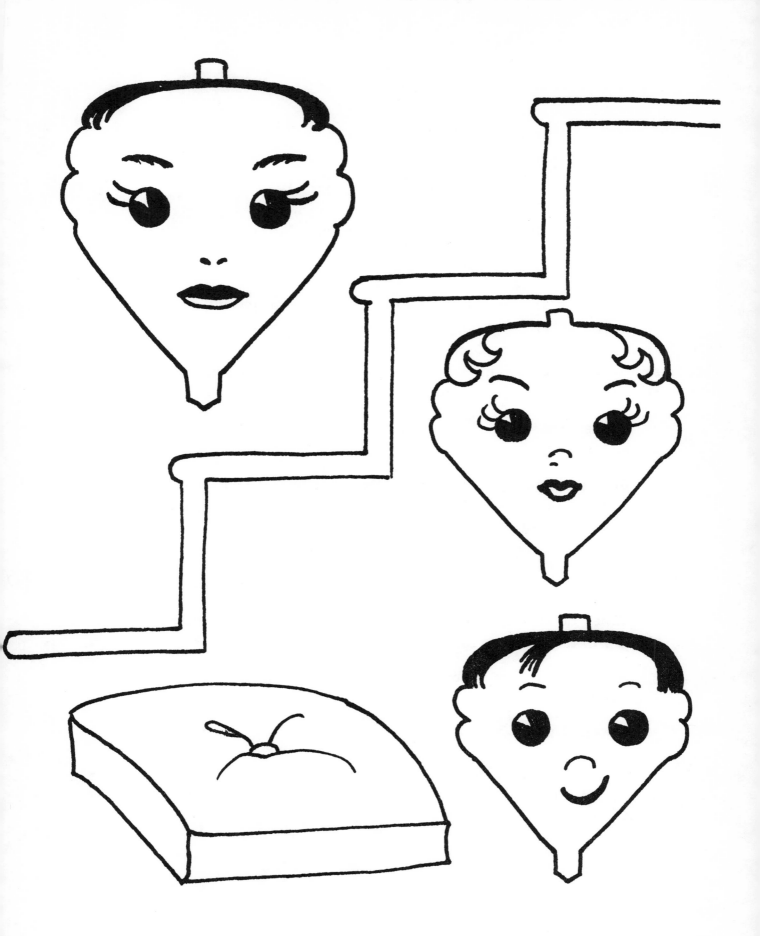

The Jingle Bells

BY MINNIE HILL, *Kindergarten Teacher, National City, Calif.*

Way up at the top of a church steeple, a man was pulling a rope to sound the bell. The bell went ding-dong, ding-dong. It was almost Christmas, and time to call all the people in the town to come to church. Suddenly, the man saw two little bells lying in a corner next to the big church bell. He picked them up and shook them. Then he listened very hard.

"These don't ding-dong like my church bell," he said, "but I will take them to someone who needs them."

So the bellman put the little bells in his pocket and went to the firehouse. He showed them to the fireman, who took them and shook them and listened very hard.

"These don't clang-clang like the bell on my fire engine," said the fireman.

"They don't ding-dong like the church bell, either," said the bellman, "but I will take them to someone who needs them."

So he took the bells home to his wife. She took them and shook them and listened very hard.

"These bells don't br-ring br-ring like my telephone bell," she said.

"And they don't ding-dong like the church bells or clang-clang like the fire engine bell," said the man, "but I will take them to someone who needs them."

So the bellman climbed into his car and drove to the farmhouse. He showed the bells to the farmer who took them and shook them and listened very hard.

"These don't clink-clink like my cowbell," said the farmer.

"They don't ding-dong like the church bell, either," said the bellman. "They don't even clang-clang like the fire engine bell or br-ring br-ring like the telephone bell, but I will take them to someone who needs them."

So the bellman put the bells in his pocket and went down to the sea. He jumped into a small boat and sailed away. He sailed for many days and many nights. Every day it grew colder. Every night it grew colder. Finally he came to an island and he sailed the boat right up to it. There he saw a big man with a long white beard. He was dressed all in red. The bellman showed the bells to the big man and said, "These little bells don't ding-dong like the church bell, or clang-clang like the fire engine bell, or br-ring br-ring like the telephone bell, or clink-clink like the cowbell, and I want to give them to someone who needs them."

The big man took the bells and shook them, and listened very hard. Then he laughed and laughed and said, "I have been looking all over the world for these bells. I need them to ride in my sleigh tonight and sing to all the children that Christmas is here. I am Santa Claus, and do you know what these bells are? They . . . are . . . the jingle bells!"

Make two

246

The Smiths' Christmas

BY MINNIE HILL, *Kindergarten Teacher, National City, Calif.*

This is Sally and Cecil's Christmas tree. They decorated it about a week ago and here it stands shining in all its beauty.

My, what a busy time. Everyone has been bustling around for days—shopping, wrapping gifts, mailing packages, baking cookies, buying trees and trimming them.

Everything seems to be ready. It should be ready because it is Christmas Eve. Mother, Father, Cecil, and Sally are in bed. So is Spot, their dog.

"I believe the Smiths are asleep," says Santa, as down the chimney he comes with a boom. He peeks around. He doesn't hear a sound so he steps out into the room.

"What a beautiful tree Cecil and Sally have," he says, as he reaches for his book. He opens it. Yes, here is the list of gifts he has brought for the Smiths—Mr. Smith, Mrs. Smith, Sally Smith, and Cecil Smith.

From his bag he pulls out a present for Daddy. They are something Daddy can wear and they begin with the sound "s." Can you guess what they are? (After the children guess "socks," place the socks under the tree.) He has something more for Daddy. It also begins with the sound "s," and Daddy will use it when he builds a doghouse for Spot. (The children guess "saw." Place the saw under the tree.)

Now he gets something out of the bag for Mother. It starts with the "s" sound and Mother will use it when she makes Sally's dress. (Scissors.)

Another gift for Mother, starting with "s" is something Mother will wear when her feet feel tired. (Slippers.)

Now he gets Sally's gifts. One that starts with "s" will keep Sally warm. She will button it down the front. (Sweater.) The next three presents are too hard to guess so I'll tell you. Santa puts a pretty dress, six silver spoons and a nurse's set under the tree for Sally.

Here are Cecil's presents. Here is a sailor suit just like Daddy's. See if you can guess these. One has two wheels and Cecil will ride it on the sidewalk. It starts with "s." (Scooter.) Another gift starting with "s" rolls and there is one for each foot. It begins with "s." (Skates.)

Santa has finished and he looks at all the gifts under the tree. He feels certain every one of the Smiths will be very happy on Christmas Day. So up the chimney he goes.

Soon it is morning. Cecil and Sally rush into the living room. Mother and Daddy follow. Cecil find his ——— (children name gifts as teacher removes Cecil's gifts from the tree—sailor suit, scooter, skates).

Sally find her ——— (sweater, nurse's set, six silver spoons, dress).

Mother finds her ——— (scissors and slippers).

Daddy finds his ——— (saw, socks).

Do you think the Smiths had a happy Christmas?

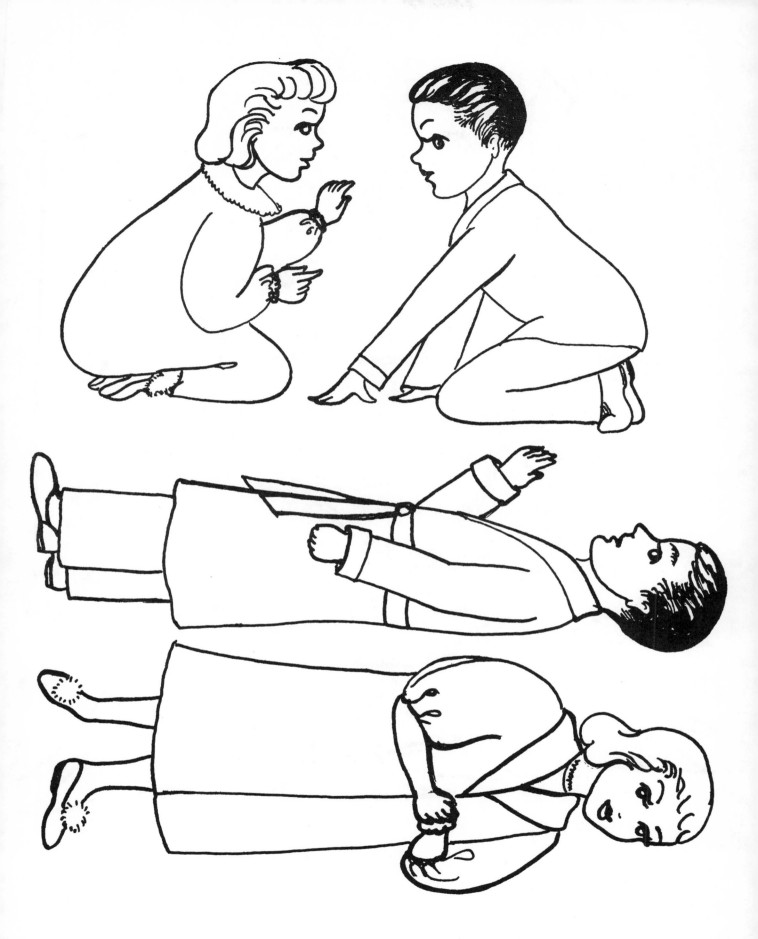

250

The Mouse and the Thunder

UNKNOWN

(Needed: Mouse, clouds, frog, duck.)

Once there was a little mouse who was afraid of thunder. When she saw thick dark clouds in the sky she would run and hide.

"Thunder! Thunder scares you!" the other mice would cry. They would chase her and cry, "Thunder! Thunder! Run!" And it scared the little mouse so she ran and hid.

One day she went for a long walk. She was far, far away. It was hot. "I'm thirsty," said the mouse. "Oh, I want a drink. I am so thirsty!" Just then it began to thunder but the little mouse was so thirsty that for a moment she didn't hear the thunder. Then a great thunder rolled out of the sky. It scared her and she cried and began to run. Then she saw a frog.

"Thunder!" he said. "I'm glad. Now my pool won't dry up." The frog liked thunder.

Then she saw a duck. "Thunder! Hurrah!" he said. "Mud is nice." The duck liked thunder.

"Why, they are glad it thunders," said the mouse. She thought and thought, "I know! When it thunders we have rain," she thought, "and rain is good. If it rains, I can have some water. And I'm so thirsty!"

The mouse was right. Soon it rained. She got her drink of water and thunder didn't scare her after that.

252

Davy Crockett and the Bear

BY BARBARA OGLESBY

I'll bet you don't know how Davy Crockett learned to grin at bears. It all started back when Davy was a little boy and loved to play in the woods. Davy tried to imitate every sound he heard in the woods. He heard the green snake slide along and say, "Ssssss, sssss," and Davy played "I'm a ssss-snake. I'm a ssss-snake. Hear me sssss, hear me sssss!"

He heard the frog saying, "Ccc-roak, ccc-roak," and Davy played "I'm a frog, I'm a frog. Hear me ccc-roak, hear me ccc-roak."

He heard the black crow as he flew and said, "Caw, caw," and Davy played "I'm a crow, I'm a crow. Hear me caw, hear me caw."

He heard the woodpecker knock on the wood with his bill, "Rrrat-tat-tat-tat, rrat-tat-tat-tat," and he said, "I'm a woodpecker, I'm a woodpecker. Hear me rrrat-tat-tat-tat, hear me rrrat-tat-tat-tat!"

He learned to make the sounds so well that when you heard a "Ssssss, sssss," you were not sure if it was Davy or a snake. And if you heard "Ccc-roak, ccc-roak," you didn't know if it was a frog or Davy. If you heard "Caw-caw," it might be Davy or it might be a crow. And if you heard "Rrrat-tat-tat-tat, rrrat-tat-tat-tat," it probably was a woodpecker, but it might be Davy.

One day Davy was out in the woods when something brown and furry came along. Can you guess what it was? Well, it said, "Grrrr." You say, "grrrr," and see what it sounds like. "Grrrr!" You're right—it was a bear. Davy wasn't a bit afraid of that bear. He started walking toward it. Guess what the bear said, "Grrrr, grrrr." That pleased Davy, so to be polite, he answered back, "Grrrr, grrrr." This surprised the bear, but he didn't want Davy to come any closer, so he took a breath and growled very loudly, "Grrrr, grrrr!" Davy thought this was so funny, he growled right back, "Grrrr, grrrr."

The bear was mad so he bared his teeth like this, and growled, "Grrr, grrr." Davy was so amused, he laughed out loud. He thought the bear was grinning at him, so he bared his teeth like this, just like the bear, and growled, "Grrrrrr, grrrrrr." That bear was so upset by Davy grinning at him that he turned and ran away.

Davy said, "I'm a bear, I'm a bear. Hear me grrrr, hear me grrrr." And that's how Davy Crockett learned to grin at bears.

The Washing Machine Story

BY MARY SHERMAN KNAPP

"Sigh-saw, sigh-saw, sigh-saw," said the washing machine. "I wish I had someone to go with me."

"I will keep you company," said the water to the washing machine. "I will fill you to the top and together we will say, 'Swish-swash, swish-swash, come and join the wash.'"

"So-sue, so-sue, so-sue," said the soap. "I wish I had someone to keep me company."

"Swish-swash, swish-swash, swish-swash, come and join the wash," said the washing machine and water to the soap. "We will make bubbles out of your soap."

"Bly-blue, bly-blue, bly-blue," said the blueing. "I wish I had someone to keep me company."

"Swish-swash, swish-swash, swish-swash, come and join the wash," said the washing machine, the water and the soap. "We shall use you, blueing, to keep the colors in the clothes nice and bright."

"Zi-zee, zi-zee, zi-zee," said the skirt with the zipper. "We wish we had someone to go with us."

"Swish-swash, swish-swash, swish-swash, come and join the wash," said the washing machine, the water, the soap, and the blueing. "We promise to keep the zipper on your skirt."

"Show-sure, show-sure, show-sure," said the shirt with the buttons. "We wish that we had someone to go with us."

"Swish-swash, swish-swash, swish-swash, come and join the wash," said the washing machine, the water, the soap, the blueing, and the skirt with the zipper. "We promise to keep the buttons on your shirt."

"Dry-dray, dry-dray, dry-dray," said the little red dress. "I wish I had someone to keep me company."

"Swish-swash, swish-swash, swish-swash, come and join the wash," said the washing machine, the soap, the blueing, the skirt with the zipper, the shirt with the buttons. "We promise to keep your dress bright red."

"See-say, see-say, see-say," said the pair of little brown socks. "We wish we had someone to go with us."

"Swish-swash, swish-swash, swish-swash, come and join the wash," said the washing machine, the water, the soap, the blueing, the skirt with the zipper, the shirt with the buttons, and the little red dress. "We promise to get your heels and toes clean." And that's the story of the washing machine!

SUGGESTIONS:

Use a flannel board and colored construction paper. Cut out a washing machine with a window visible in the front, a box of soap, bottle of blueing, skirt, shirt, dress and socks.

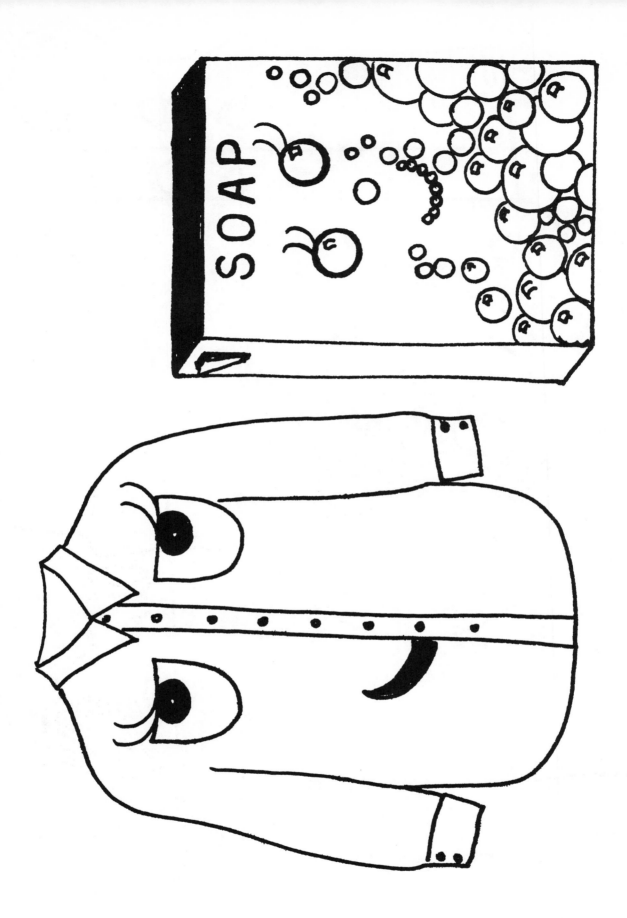

The Rickety Rick Fence

BY MARY SHERMAN KNAPP

Once there was a farmer with a fence. (Place construction paper fence on flannel board.) One day the farmer went out to the fence and leaned against it. The fence went, "Rickety-rick, rickety-rick, rickety-rick."

"Well," said the farmer, "that fence has a loose nail in it. I'll go back to the farmhouse and get my toolbox and fix it." The farmer brought his best hammer back to fix the fence.

He was all ready to pound the loose nail back in the fence when along came a bumblebee. "Z-z-z-z-z-z--z." (Flannel board bee lights right on the fence.) "Well," said the farmer, "I can't pound the nail back in the fence now. The bumblebee might get mad and go, 'Z-z-z-z-z-z-z-z' (storyteller motions possible movement of bee from fence to his face, stopping 'Z-z-z-z-z-z-z' suddenly) and sting me. I'd better wait."

Along came a cow. "Moo, moo, moo, moo." She was looking for grass and leaned against the fence. "Rickety-rick, rickety-rick, rickety-rick," went the fence. Pretty soon the cow moved away from the fence to stand in the grass.

Then came the pig. "Oink, oink, oink, oink." The pig leaned hard against the fence. "Rickety-rick, rickety-rick, rickety-rick," went the fence. This made the farmer mad. He turned to the pig and said, "Shoo, shoo" (say the aforementioned in a rather fast, disgruntled manner). "Oink, oink, oink, oink," went the pig, and he moved away from the fence.

There was a snake moving through the grass. That snake had all the time in the world. He had no place to go and was taking all afternoon getting there. Slowly and quietly, he said, "S-s-s-s-s-s-s-s." Then he stopped in the grass to rest.

Suddenly, a blowfly flew through the air, "V-vv, v-vv, v-vv." Then he settled down on the other end of the fence. (Place him on the opposite end of the fence from the bumblebee.) When the bumblebee saw the blowfly, he wanted to get a closer look at him. So he went, "Z-z-z-z-z-z-z," and buzzed over to the blowfly. Well, the blowfly didn't like this one bit. He went, "V-vv, v-vv," and flew away. The bumblebee decided to follow him, "Z-z-z-z-z-z-z," and off he went after the blowfly.

The cow, who had been chewing her cud quietly, decided to walk out in the pasture. "Moo, moo, moo, moo."

By this time, the pig decided he was hungry and would go back to the pigpen to see if there were any food. You know how pigs are—hungry all the time, "Oink, oink, oink, oink."

But that snake, it had all the time in the world. There was no place in particular to go and no hurry to get there. The sun felt so warm and good. (Slowly and quietly, "S-s-s-s-s-s-s-s.")

"Now," said the farmer, "I can pound that loose nail back in the fence."

"Pound, pound, pound," went the farmer's hammer. Finally, the farmer pulled the fence, pushed the fence, leaned up against the fence. But the fence didn't go "Rickety-rick, rickety-rick, rickety-rick" any more. The loose nail had been pounded back into the fence.

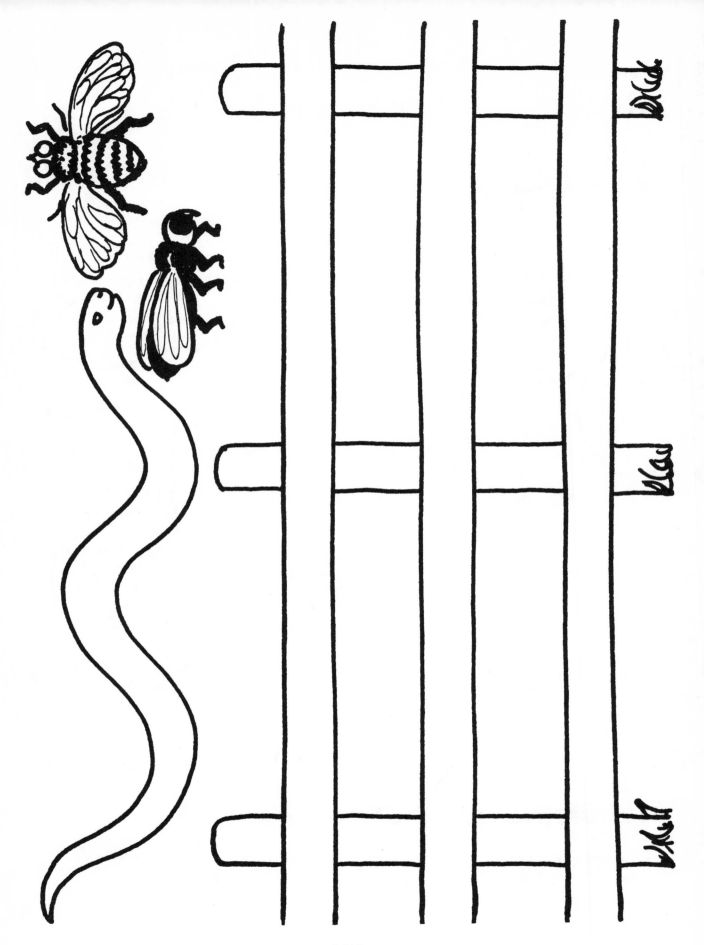

Bibliography

FLANNELGRAPH

Boggs, A. and Schofield, R. E.: "Piece of Flannel and a Bit of Imagination," *National Elementary Principal*, September 1956.

Dunser, A.: "Flanagrams," *Catholic School Journal*, March 1958.

Farrow, E.: "Flannel Board in My First Grade," *Instructor*, June 1957.

Grassell, E. M.: "Effective Flannel Boards," *Educational Screen and Audio-Visual Guide*, March 1958.

Grassell, E. M. "Flannel Boards in Action," *Educational Screen and Audio-Visual Guide*, June 1955.

Grassell, E. M.: "Flannel Boards in Elementary School," *Instructor*, May 1956.

Grassell, E. M.: "Use Flannel Boards for Better Teaching," *Clearing House*, March 1956.

Hoffman, H. W.: "Flannelgraph Fun," *Education Music Magazine*, January 1955.

Hoffman, H. W.: "Flannelgraph for Hansel and Gretel," *Education Music Magazine*, March 1956.

Howitt, L.: "Flannel Board in Social Studies," *High Points*, April 1958.

Long, P. E.: "Teaching with the Flannel Board," Jaconda Manufacturing Company, 5449 Hunte Street, Philadelphia 31, Pa.

Manning, D. S.: "Handy Flannel Board," *Grade Teacher*, October 1958.

Osborn, M. P.: "Flannel Board," M. P. Osborn, Box 3, Redlands, Calif.

Pennington, L. B.: "For Your Flannel Board," *Instructor*, June 1959.

Sands, L. B.: "Flannel Boards," *Grade Teacher*, February 1957.

Walter, B.: "Let's Dust Off Our Flannelgraphs," *Grade Teacher*, March 1957.

FILMS

Flannelgraph. 27 minutes. Color. ESC 467. University of Minnesota, Minneapolis, Minn.

Flannel Boards and How to Use Them. 15 minutes. Color. ESC 516. Bailey Films.

EQUIPMENT

Jacronda Manufacturing Co., 1635 N. 55th Street, Philadelphia 31, Pa.

Kenworthy Education Service, 138 Allen Street, Buffalo 1, New York.

Dennison Company, Framingham, Mass.

Ann Marie's Workshop, 6048 Avondale Avenue, Chicago 31, Ill.

Palfrey's School Supply Co., 7549 E. Garvey Blvd., San Gabriel, Calif.

Gel-Sten Supply Co., 944 South Hill St., Los Angeles 15, Calif.

STORYTELLING

Bailey, C. S.: *For the Story Teller*, Milton Bradley, Springfield, 1915.

Duff, A.: *Bequest of Wings*, Viking Press, New York, 1954.

Cundiff, R. E. and Webb, B.: *Storytelling for You*, Antioch Press, 1917.

Horne, H. H.: *Storytelling, Questioning and Studying*, MacMillan, Yellow Springs, Ohio, 1957.

Larrick, Nancy: *Teacher's Guide to Children's Books*, Charles E. Merrill, Columbus, Ohio, 1960.

Miller, G. T.: *Storytelling to Live Wire Boys*, E. P. Dutton, New York, 1930.

Sawyer, Ruth: *The Way of the Story Teller*, Viking, New York, 1957.

Shedlock, M. L.: *The Art of the Storyteller*, Dover Publishing Company, 1951.

Tooze, Ruth: *Storytelling*, Prentice Hall, New York, 1959.

Ward, M.: *Young Minds Need Something to Grow On*, Row Peterson Company, Evanston, Illinois, 1957.

Wagner, J. A. and Smith, R. W.: *Teacher's Guide to Storytelling*, W. C. Brown, Dubuque, Iowa, 1958.

Arbuthnot, M. H.: *Art of Story Telling*, Conference on Reading, Pittsburgh University, 1957.

Fenner, P. R.: "Why Tell Stories," *Elementary English*, March 1957.

Martin, W.: *And Now the Storyteller Comes*, Reading Conference, Syracuse University, 1960.

Martin, W.: "Some Stories Should Be Memorized," *Elementary English*, March 1957.

Nees, R. B.: "Needed Storytellers," *Teachers College Journal*, January 1955.

Rollins, C.: "Storytelling: Its Value and Importance," *Elementary English*, March 1957.

Teaney, V.: "Storytelling Techniques," *Practical Home Economics*, December 1957.

Waugh, D.: "Pre-Kindergarten Story Hour," *Wilson Library Bulletin*, April 1959.